Leadership Vitality

A Workbook for Academic Administrators

Leadership Vitality

A Workbook for Academic Administrators

By David G. Brown
Provost and Executive Vice President
for Academic Affairs, Miami University

AMERICAN COUNCIL ON EDUCATION
WASHINGTON, D.C.

© 1979 by the American Council on Education
One Dupont Circle, Washington, D.C. 20036

Library of Congress Cataloging in Publication Data
Brown, David G
    Leadership vitality.

    Based on information gathered from the
Leadership Vitality Project.
        1. College administrators—United States.
2. Leadership.   I.   Title.
LB2341.B668   378.1′1′0973   79-23037
ISBN 0-8268-1331-3

9 8 7 6 5 4 3 2 1

Contents

Preface

In June 1978, I wrote letters to sixty college and university presidents and chief academic officers, challenging them to join me in a Leadership Vitality Project. To my amazement, fifty-one said yes.

The premise for the project, and the workbook, is that professional vitality is best promoted by sharing information with colleagues in the professional group. During the past year, presidents and chief academic officers—the fifty-one and many others (see list below)—have interviewed each other, convened in two-hour workshops at several national meetings, and joined in a three-day Leadership Vitality Conference. The many quotations throughout the workbook are drawn from project activities.

For me, the Leadership Vitality Project has been invigorating and reassuring. The presidents and chief academic officers of our nation's colleges and universities seem to be selflessly committed to quality education. They believe that they are making real differences for the better. The many leaders touched by this project willingly admitted their personal need to continue growing and have committed their time and dollars to finding new answers. They are at once humble and self-assured, seeking and leading, discouraged and optimistic, inadequately prepared and competent.

Leaders do make a difference. Who is president, who is dean, does matter. Much poor-mouthing and hand-holding occurs when presidents talk to one another about their frustrations, be the topic a tenured faculty, an unenlightened board, overzealous football fans, misintentioned bureaucrats, or fickle students. A chronicle of the anecdotes shared in the corridors of national gatherings would suggest a feeling of power-lessness, of impotency, of nonachievement throughout the ranks of college presidents.

The poor-mouthing is only a pretense. Presidents may have less power than they wish, less than in the past, less than they need to achieve their vision in a timely manner. The interviews show clearly, however, that presidents know their offices are the focal point for getting things done. They quickly volunteer long lists of achievements, large and small, when asked, "What are two or three of your proudest achievements since assuming office?" Throughout, they show great optimism about the ability of quality leaders to make crucial decisions.

The honing of leadership skills, the continued renewal of the desire and the capacity to lead, the search for one's strengths and weaknesses, and the charting of personal development all begin with the belief that how well one performs does, and will, make a difference.

Acknowledgments

The time frame of this project has been unreal. So many people have been so accommodating—and so quick to respond.

Just one year ago, owing largely to persistent encouragement by Peggy Heim (senior research officer of TIAA-CREF) and the commitment of the interviewers to volunteer their own time and travel expenses, Carnegie Corporation of New York took only three weeks to decide to fund incidental expenses and the distribution of this workbook to all college presidents. With only four weeks' notice, Frederic W. Ness, director, Presidential Search Consultation Service, Association of American Colleges; John W. Nason, director, Study of Presidential Selection and Assessment, Association of Governing Boards; Donald E. Walker, president, Southeastern Massachusetts University; and Arlon E. Elser, program director, W. K. Kellogg Foundation, joined the project interviewers to design the questionnaire. President J. W. Peltason and W. Todd Furniss, senior academic adviser, of the American Council on Education agreed to cosponsor the Leadership Vitality Conference in only two weeks.

While E. Alden Dunham, Carnegie program officer, and Karen Egan, Carnegie program associate, were expediting final release of the workbook funding, the ACE publications department staff members were lending their magic touch so that the manuscript could move from draft to publication in less than three months. On so many occasions, my colleagues at Miami University, especially Bill Hanger and Sandra Packard, were coordinating and commenting on each part of the project. Colleagues at Miami (Derrell Hart, Rebecca Lukens, Charles Teckman, Karl Schilling, Charles Skipper, Judith George, Douglas Reed, Tom Dority, Don Auble, Diane Devestern, Ted Wagenaar, and Roy Ward) and a group of student leaders helped survey the leadership literature. Most of all, Mary

Ellers, secretary to the provost, turned impossible deadlines into completions.

The key contributors were, of course, the interviewers and the interviewees. They are the true authors of this volume, and to many of them I am indebted for permission to draw on their materials.

Participants in interviews and roundtables

Martin G. Abegg, President, Bradley University
Alfred H. Adams, President, Broward Community College
Daniel G. Aldrich, Chancellor, University of California—Irvine
Peter H. Armacost, President, Eckerd College
Robert G. Arns, Vice President for Academic Affairs, University of Vermont
Jay Barton II, Vice President and Provost for Academic Affairs, West Virginia University (now President, University of Alaska)
A. B. Bonds, Jr., President, Baldwin Wallace College
Neil S. Bucklew, Provost, Ohio University
L. Leon Campbell, Provost, University of Delaware
Lisle C. Carter, President, University of the District of Columbia—Van Ness
A. Ray Chamberlain, President, Colorado State University
George C. Christensen, Vice President for Academic Affairs, Iowa State University
Martha E. Church, President, Hood College
James M. Clark, Vice President for Academic Affairs, University of Maine (now President, SUNY College at Cortland)
David M. Clarke, S.J., President, Regis Educational Corporation
Lattie F. Coor, President, University of Vermont
Thomas A. Davis, Dean of the University, University of Puget Sound
Archie R. Dykes, Chancellor, University of Kansas
David W. Ellis, President, Lafayette College
William R. Ferrante, Vice President for Academic Affairs, University of Rhode Island
Michael R. Ferrari, Provost, Bowling Green State University
J. Thomas Finucan, President, Viterbo College
Porter L. Fortune, Jr., Chancellor, University of Mississippi
Anne Fuller, Dean of the Faculty, Scripps College
James Furman, Executive Director, Illinois Board of Higher Education
David P. Gardner, President, University of Utah
Louis C. Gatto, President, Marian College
Melvin D. George, Vice President for Academic Affairs, University of Missouri
James F. Gollattscheck, President, Valencia Community College
Nancie L. Gonzalez, Vice Chancellor for Academic Affairs, University of Maryland—College Park
Norman Hackerman, President, Rice University
Paul Hardin, President, Drew University
Charles L. Hayes, President, Albany State College

Keith Spalding, President, Franklin and Marshall College
Roberta Stewart, Dean of the College, Hollins College
Joab L. Thomas, Chancellor, North Carolina State University
Robert E. L. Strider II, President, Colby College
Arnold G. Tew, Vice President, Cleveland State University
Franklin W. Wallin, President, Earlham College
Lloyd I. Watkins, President, Illinois State University
George B. Weathersby, Commissioner, State of Indiana Commission for Higher
    Education
Thomas E. Wenzlau, President, Ohio Wesleyan University
Harold B. Whiteman, Jr., President, Sweet Briar College
Nash N. Winstead, Provost and Vice Chancellor, North Carolina State University
Robert E. Wolverton, Vice President for Academic Affairs, Mississippi State
    University
Lloyd E. Worner, President, Colorado College

Participants in the Leadership Vitality Conference

David W. Benson, Vice President for Academic Affairs, California State University—
    Northridge
A. Paul Bradley, Jr., Associate Provost, New York Institute of Technology,
    Metropolitan Center
James L. Chapman, President, West Liberty State College
James M. Clark, President-designate, SUNY College at Cortland
Barbara Crawford, Academic Dean, Wood Junior College
Edwin W. Crooks, Chancellor, Indiana University Southeast
Wayne E. Culp, Academic Dean, Spartanburg Methodist College
Thomas A. Davis, Dean, University of Puget Sound
James Ebben, Dean, Siena Heights College
DeBow Freed, President, Monmouth College
W. Todd Furniss, Senior Academic Adviser, American Council on Education
Robert J. Garrity, Vice President for Academic and Student Affairs, Saint Joseph's
    College
Sr. Madelein Sophie Hebert, President, Our Lady of Holy Cross College
Victor Hurst, Vice President for Academic Affairs, Clemson University
Larry A. Jackson, President, Lander College
Charles J. Keffer, Vice President for Academic Affairs, College of St. Thomas
G. Benjamin Lantz, Dean, Mount Union College
Sharon MacLaren, Academic Dean, Saint Joseph College
Neal Malicky, Vice President for Academic Affairs and Dean of College, Baldwin-
    Wallace College
Pressley McCoy, President, Dayton-Miami Valley Consortium
Mary S. Metz, Provost and Dean of Academic Affairs, Hood College
John D. Millett, Executive Vice President and Director, Management and Finance
    Programs, Academy for Educational Development, Inc.
Joseph Mills, President, Gaston College

Edward O'Keefe, Academic Dean and Acting President, Niagara City Community College

Samuel Rankin, Dean of Academic Affairs, Valley City State College

David L. Rice, President, Indiana State University—Evansville Campus

John T. Richardson, Executive Vice President and Dean of Faculties, DePaul University

Cornelius Robbins, Associate Chancellor—Community Colleges, State University of New York

James L. Talbot, Vice President for Academic Affairs and Provost, Western Washington University

Stephen Joel Trachtenberg, President, University of Hartford

Franklin W. Wallin, President, Earlham College

Robert Wittman, Vice President for Academic Affairs, Bellarmine College

Even as I accept full responsibility for this volume—and reemphasize that the views are not necessarily those of either the Carnegie Corporation or of the American Council on Education—I gratefully acknowledge the substantial and prompt contributions of each agency and each person to this venture. All of us have grown, but the greatest benefit and pleasure have been mine.

Chapter One

The Workbook

This workbook is for college and university executives who seek new ideas, self-improvement and revitalization, and institutional renewal. It is based on the following propositions:

- Leaders learn best from colleagues; for example, college presidents can learn by swapping experiences with other presidents. The words of corporate executives and of scholars of administration may be less pertinent to the job at hand than the advice of a respected and trusted executive at a comparable college or university.
- Ideas from colleagues can spark new ideas, new thoughts. The ideas of others are thought-*starters* and are more often built upon than mimicked.
- Interviews and other communication techniques can stimulate meaningful discussion among colleagues. The corridor conversations at professional meetings are too often brief and shallow.
- Leaders can improve their skills and job performance by reading, studying, and using this workbook. Although they should not expect radical transformations, they may glean helpful tips, clarify personal values, discover one or two implementation strategies, map a personal development plan, encourage other leaders toward self-development, or begin to think about leadership in new ways.

The quotations in the workbook are drawn from interviews, workshops, and meetings conducted as part of the Leadership Vitality Project. The project has five parts:

1. *Interviews.* Fifty-two presidents and chief academic officers agreed to interview one or two colleague presidents or chief academic officers of their own choosing. The three-hour interviews, usually conducted at professional meetings, employed an interview guide (Appendix A) derived from hypotheses on leadership submitted by interviewers (Appendix B). Decision-making principles, implementation strategies, techniques for keeping professionally fresh, leadership attributes, and "tips to colleagues" were the focus of the questions.

The interviewers, with a single exception, have all been chief executive officers or chief academic officers for at least three years and came from a diversity of institutions: 63 percent, presidents; 62 percent from the public sector; 58 percent from universities; 36 percent from four-year colleges; and 6 percent from two-year colleges. Thirty-eight percent came from the East; 44 percent from the Midwest; and 18 percent from the West. Thirteen percent, women; and ten percent, blacks.

The interviewees were equally diverse: 87 percent, presidents and chancellors. Forty-nine percent from the public sector; 54 percent from universities; 41 percent from four-year colleges; and 5 percent from two-year colleges. Forty-four percent came from the East; 41 percent from the Midwest; and 15 percent from the West. All persons interviewed had been chief executive officers or chief academic officers for at least three years, with the average length of service just over nine years. Seventeen percent were under forty-six years old; 40 percent, forty-six to fifty-five; 40 percent, fifty-six to sixty-five; and 3 percent, sixty-six or older.

2. *Roundtables.* All participants were invited to attend swap-and-share sessions held in conjunction with the annual meetings of the American Council on Education, the National Association of Land-Grant Colleges and Universities, the Association of American Colleges, and the American Association for Higher Education. Each roundtable attracted from ten to twenty-five participants.

Participants were asked to bring copies of two documents or statements they thought would interest colleagues. For example, participants in the AAC roundtable were asked to bring a one-page "statement of the educational principle that dominates your decision making" and a copy of the "instrument used in your institution for evaluating administrators." Each person was given five to ten minutes for presentation and discussion. Topics at other roundtables have included resource allocation, time management, academic planning, delegation, relations with the board, and the meaning of a "sense of direction."

3. *Leadership Vitality Conference.* On June 17–20, 1979, in Oxford, Ohio, thirty-two chief academic officers and chief executive officers interviewed each other, participated in roundtable discussions, and heard a preliminary summary of the nationally conducted interviews. The conference, jointly sponsored by the American Council on Education, Miami University (Ohio), and Carnegie Corporation of New York, was billed as "a self-development project for academic leaders ... a way for college presidents and chief academic officers to learn from each other, to share ideas, develop trust, and talk over common problems." Rated by

two presidents as "the best I've ever attended" and judged by all as a superior learning experience, the conference closely followed the format suggested in chapter 6.

4. *Workshops.* Planned are several one-day workshops at national meetings of college and university presidents and chief academic officers. The workshops will be open to conference registrants, probably at a nominal additional charge. The procedures and techniques described here are intended to encourage other persons and groups to offer workshops.

5. *The Workbook.* The workbook is principally a compendium of quotations on leadership, by leaders. The concepts and principles, the strategies and techniques, the shortcuts and tips, are compiled under five chapter headings: Decision-making Principles, Implementation Strategies, Revitalization Strategies, Leadership Profiles, and Professional Renewal Strategies. Chapters 2−5 include brief overviews of leadership topics, a selection of quotations highlighting responses by chief executive officers and chief academic officers, and lists of follow-up exercises and activities. Chapter 6 describes how readers can develop leadership vitality projects for themselves and for their associates. Appendix A is the interview guide and questionnaire used by interviewers to collect responses. Appendix B is a list of hypotheses, from letters and the literature, on the qualities of an effective leader.

Persons who intend to read or study the workbook should read the chapters in order. However, to gain the greatest benefit from the workbook, readers should first answer the questions in the interview guide or—better still—have a trusted colleague interview them. In either case, readers should compile a list of "things to do and think about" before proceeding to chapter 2.

Remember, the purpose of the workbook is not to describe good leadership but to help develop it.

Chapter Two

Decision-making Principles

Leaders must have guiding principles, but principles are rarely articulated in a form conducive to study, mimicking, or learning. Far more frequent than the suggestion of an appropriate principle is the exhortation about the importance of decision making based in principle. In fact, there are many useful principles, each expressible in many ways. And the principle useful for one circumstance is often inappropriate for other places, times, and people.

This chapter focuses on The Principle, presenting statements of chief executive officers and chief academic officers on their primary vision: the ideal, the first principles, the fundamental concepts to which most of the important decisions can be traced. These are the big ideas that are used to measure the wisdom of virtually every decision made—budget decisions, time decisions, personnel decisions, policy decisions. Some principles mentioned here are contradictory; no person could possibly adopt them all. Rather, the principles are presented with the hope that readers may identify the principles that guide and influence *their* decisions.

Having a principle that informs most of our decisions lends integrity to them. From the principle comes consistency; from consistency comes credibility. Credible leaders have more followers and probably get more done than leaders who fall short on this score.

Knowing the principle—being aware of it—promotes its consistent application. The flow of decisions is smooth. The leader who knows the principle can deduce what actions to initiate and is not merely a responder to the initiatives of others.

Articulating the principle enables a leader to set guidelines within which others may make delegated decisions. Desires can be more readily communicated to associates, so that decisions made throughout even a complex organization can be guided by the same principle.

For example, basing decisions on a belief that learning is enhanced when teacher and learner trust the sincerity and ability of each other means that decisions as disparate as academic calendar, residence hall construction, promotion in rank, and computerization of student records have a common theme: trust. *Knowing* that the "Trust Principle" is primary allows the decision maker to ask what changes should be considered in the physical plant, budget-making process, student registration system, and hiring strategy. By *articulating* the trust principle, the leader lets associates know that ideas and proposals which enhance trustful relationships are favored for adoption. Associates are then more likely to present ideas that correctly interpret the leader's intentions.

Having, knowing, and articulating basic concepts and principles is important:

"A leader should set goals and then test every decision against them. The primary influence of a president is as planner and budgeter."
President, Midwest, Public University

"Good decision making is choosing which values to maximize, not maximizing just any value."
Vice President for Academic Affairs, Midwest, Public University

"Understand what is the *purpose*, not simply the process, involved in an action or policy."
President, East, Private College

"A leader has to be able to convey to those around him that he has a sense of vision and knows the direction in which the institution is going. ... He must be able to sift out of the variety of alternatives those which are important directions. He must see these in advance. He must be able to predict problem areas and the forces and winds of change. If he cannot do this, he and his institution will be off balance. It is like steering a ship and keeping it on course."
President, South, Public University

"Effective leadership involves knowing where you are headed, having principles, and then following them."
20-year President, East, Private College

"Effective leadership is the ability to achieve consensus on the mission, goals, and objectives of an institution and then, by working through others, to proceed to achieve the mission, goals, and objectives in an orderly and effective fashion."
President, East, Community College

"A leader must have a vision which provides a reason for decisions. That is, there must be a framework for decisions and an objective in his hopes for accomplishments. That objective must be related to higher education, to educational purposes. There simply has to be a reason for actions."
President, Midwest, Public University

Leaders Speak

When pressed to respond, most executives were able to articulate a single concept that has helped them make many different types of decisions. The concepts themselves are almost as diverse as the executives and their institutions. Fourteen concepts are presented as illustrations.

1. Centrality of learning

"The central purpose of the president is to make a place where students and faculty learn. ... The academic program is the only reason the place is here. ... The heart and soul of an educational institution is dedicated to learning. Teaching responsibility must remain the most important function of the institution. Dollars on administration must be minimized. The faculty must not vacate its responsibility for the education of the whole student and thereby allow a dissipation of funds to support staff, especially in the student affairs area."
20-year President, South, Private University

"To participate in the academy, whether as student, teacher, or administrator, is a privilege and a lofty responsibility. To participate in the academy is to perpetuate and enhance the richest experiences of humankind and to open new vistas for our future. ... Education is an experience in dialogue in which limitations of time and space are transcended and new experiences of relationship and identity occur. The teacher and the student engage in conversations with each other and with their counterparts elsewhere in time and space. The struggles and victories of others are ours, and their support is strangely with us in our struggles—their joy enriches our victories. To strive for excellence, on the other hand, is at once an enhancement of our own life, a fulfillment of the lives that preceded us in the academy (broadly conceived) and the laying of a foundation for those that follow. Our purpose is the same as that of W. H. Auden's Wise Men—

to discover how to be human. So perceived, education is not a temporary hurdle to be cleared but an enduring experience to be cherished. We must not let it be seen as anything less!"
Vice President for Academic Affairs, Midwest, Private College

2. Rational civility

"The university must protect and extend, must advocate and practice, civil dialogue. Polemics should be avoided. Shared respect, shared language, shared dialogue—these are the best logical and stylistic characteristics of the university. Conversations within the university should accomplish larger purposes and reflect the culture as a whole. There should exist mutual understanding and a sense of community. Dialogue should not only be advocated by the university but also practiced in domains such as governance procedure."
Vice President for Academic Affairs, Midwest, Public University

3. Trust theory

"Students grow most when they trust their environment. They must believe that their professors are up-to-date and care, recognize their university as a place of quality, find exemplars they wish to emulate, have available the books, journals, and instrumentation appropriate for the time. Students and faculty should know one another's integrity, sincerity, earnestness. The propensity of students to risk new beliefs increases greatly when their mentors are experts who care. The educating objective of the university can best be fulfilled by creating an environment replete with trust. . . . This philosophy influences hiring strategies, choice of academic calendars, emphasis upon cocurricular programming, publicity of faculty achievements, stroking of faculty, registration policy, etc."
Vice President for Academic Affairs, Midwest, Public University

"It is my belief that change and consideration of change are accomplished best if the person responsible has the respect of the people he works with and, in turn, respects them."
President, East, Public University

"Students learn best in an atmosphere of trust, an environment free of the mediocrity syndrome."
President, South, Private College

4. *Infectious enthusiasm*

Participants in a Leadership Roundtable on Decision-making Principles were asked to bring to the meeting copies of their answer to the question, What principle informs your decision making? The first three leaders who distributed statements focused on the same point.

"There would be little disagreement that knowledge of one's field is the starting point for successful teaching. To my mind, two other ingredients mark the superior teacher: an *infectious enthusiasm* for the subject and a high demand level in what is required of students. Enthusiasm generates the learning development process; the demand level is the fixing agent."
President, South, Private College

"While learning requires solid substance—information, knowledge, defined subject matter—and is more damaging than helpful without such basic ingredients, the essential character of liberal learning lies in the 'style' of the teacher and the process by which the teacher engages students with the subject. Without this style and process, the teacher is hardly worth having present. Without the knowledge, the process becomes only a faint shadow of learning."
President, East, Private College

"A good teacher is more important than what is taught. One ought to choose a college major on the strength of the department and not on the basis of subject matter. A good teacher can serve to guide a student to a fine education regardless of major."
President, East, Private University

"A leader enjoys being involved with people who are thinking and doing. The leader's enthusiasm helps to reinforce the enthusiasm already there."
Vice President for Academic Affairs, East, Public University

5. *Access*

"The university must be an advocate and disciple of knowledge. This means demystifying knowledge for *all* members of society. It means democratization of growth opportunities. It means providing access to knowledge for all people."
Vice President for Academic Affairs, Midwest, Public University

"People have a better possibility to be better people in both a personal and practical sense with higher education. I believe in public higher education and in access."
President, Midwest, Public University

"We must extend educational opportunities to all in the community who can benefit."
President, East, Community College

"Opportunities to learn must be available to all American citizens, at all times throughout their lives."
President, East, Community College

6. *Education as servant of society*

"In education we need to ascertain the educational needs of society, how to meet them, and how to keep society recognizing what is needed. Institutional goals ought to be bound up in the needs of society."
Vice President for Academic Affairs, Midwest, Public University

"The university must seek ways to be of greater service to the state and the region."
President, Midwest, Public University

"Education is what society is about."
President, Midwest, Public University

7. *Student needs*

"The university is ... trying to be as responsive to student desires as possible."
Vice President for Academic Affairs, East, Public University

"Responsiveness to the needs of present and future students is our mission."
President, East, Private College

8. *Great research university*

"The concept of a premiere research institution is a clear sense of direction that guides my decision making."
President, South, Public University

"Certain universities are, and ought to be, the developers of new wisdom, of creative points in society. Education is a social good as well as a personal good."
President, Midwest, Public University

9. Different strokes for different folks

"Each individual is unique. Options within our educational programs must provide alternatives for all students. Each student should be pushed as far and as fast as he or she will allow."
President, South, Private College

"Each university should have an opportunity to organize its educational program to meet the unique and distinctive needs of its students."
President, Midwest, Public University

10. More talented than you think

"Most human beings are more talented than they realize. In an environment that simultaneously puts them at ease, gives them confidence, and challenges them, they can and will perform at higher levels of competence than they anticipated. This principle directs my relations with my students, faculty colleagues, staff, friends, family, and self."
Vice President for Academic Affairs, East, Private College

11. Uncertain future

"By not overplanning, unexpected opportunities can be seized and serendipity can be built into the system."
President, South, Public University

"My institution is planning for the uncertain future. We plan to maintain quality at the expense of quantity. Nevertheless, we are also cognizant of the need for contingency plans—the 'what if?' possibility. Every college president must take the worst alternative into consideration as he tries to project into the 1980s."
20-year President, Midwest, Private College

12. *Educational quality*

By far the most frequently mentioned basic principle was *quality*. Vague yet pervasive, the notion of maintaining quality dominates. It, more than any other concept, is on the minds of successful presidents when decisions are made.

"It is the responsibility of a president to emphasize traditional stands of quality and to reinstill the principles that led to the founding of a learning institution."
President, South, Private University

"Regardless of enrollment crunches, reasonable academic standards must be maintained. If one finds low-quality programs, corrections must be made or the institution must get rid of them."
Vice President for Academic Affairs, East, Public University

"The president must avoid dilutions of quality.... Sometimes the president must intervene if approvals become too sloppy."
20-year President, East, Private College

"We plan, despite the specters of 'steady state' and declining enrollments, to maintain quality at the expense of quantity."
20-year President, East, Private College

"———— University is not a place where you have to go with what is current.... Fads are for others.... Adjust the quantity, not the quality, of what we do."
President, South, Private University

"As enrollments decline, universities will redirect dollars toward serving fewer students better. The quality corners cut during expansion will be reinstated. We shall at last turn to a long list of qualitative erosions. Front-end investment in libraries will be regarded as cost effective.... Educational effectiveness will be restored as the universities once again emphasize basic skills. In sum, there will be qualitative improvements in teaching and learning."
Vice President for Academic Affairs, Midwest, Public University

"The goal of my university today is for greater institutional enhancement and for greater qualitative development of the faculty."
President, West, Public University

"Ten years ago we expected our enrollment to go to two thousand students by 1980. We have reached the goal. This was not in the best interest of the college with the resources available; hence, the goal is now fifteen hundred students. We changed our emphasis from quantitative to qualitative."
President, South, Private College

"I no longer believe that all ills are solved by growth."
President, South, Public University

13. *Liberal arts*

"The world and its people need more, not less, of the civilizing, enriching, broadening yet disciplining effects of the liberal arts and sciences, especially insomuch as they focus on mankind in all the various worlds in which we live. Other forms of educational training—professional, vocational-technical, career—are, to be sure, extremely important but should not be substituted for liberal general education. Our ultimate mission as educators must be to provide more and more of the latter to serve as the foundation, and then to provide the specialties."
President, East, Private College

"————College is a liberal arts institution, not a graduate school, not a professional school. ... Formerly, ——— College had a business administration program that had become an anomaly in a liberal arts college. I redirected the program, discouraged practical and applied courses. ... The administrative sciences program now consists mostly of courses that are theory oriented ..."
20-year President, East, Private College

"All college graduates need a core of liberal arts and humanities, regardless of the kind of institution. Human and aesthetic values are important as a basis for understanding the universe."
President, West, Public University

"Education must deal with the soul and the intangible aspects of human existence."
President, West, Public University

14. *Other principles*

"We must do only those things that we do a first-rate job at. . . . We will not try to do everything. We must capitalize on the strengths of the region. For example, the presence of the chemical industry suggests an emphasis on science, mathematics, and economic history."
Vice President for Academic Affairs, East, Public University

"We are determining what the college can do best. We cannot be all things to all people. We expect to concentrate on fewer majors, fewer students. We will do fewer things and accentuate quality consistent with resources."
President, South, Private College

"Our educational purpose is to enable students to learn how to analyze problems and to make decisions rationally. We try to get our students to identify problems, to assemble data on these problems, and to develop a thought process analyzing all data, realizing that all ideas are not of equal value. We try to get them to develop verbal and written skills that will enable them to state the problems and the data and to formulate their statements of response. Finally, we want to encourage appraisal of everyone's position."
20-year President, Midwest, Private College

"I believe the university is basically an educational institution and, as such, represents a conserving process—the need to preserve the best of what we have and to be an institution which is enabling and advancing the future of our culture and of mankind. Colleges and universities must also be renewing institutions and ones that extend to people . . ."
President, East, Public University

"My institution continues to emphasize lifelong learning opportunities for place-bound adults."
President, Midwest, Private University

"The 1980s will see universities responding to the needs of adults who enter a world of increasingly rapid change . . . with a set of skills and knowledge that will quickly become outmoded. Universities will accept the responsibility of . . . updating those skills."
Vice President for Academic Affairs, Midwest, Public University

"Building community is a goal equal in value to the goals of scholarship and service."
President, West, Private College

"The core mission of the nation's universities is to protect and enhance the knowledge resources of society.... Universities must facilitate the pursuit of truth.... recover, organize, accumulate, and disseminate knowledge. The ethical imperative ... is integrity, not popularity."
Vice President for Academic Affairs, Midwest, Public University

"One's educational philosophy is multifaceted. An important aspect of my educational philosophy ... is the necessity for the educated person to develop a sense of respect. Such respect relates to the importance of study and scholarship, to the significance of man's relationship to man and to his environment, to the value of learning in its totality, and to the development of respect for people and property. Respect is not innate but must be developed. Its absence is apparent in our time, but its return must be assured."
President, Midwest, Private College

"The university can be no better than its students and faculty. All allocations and decisions should enhance the university's ability to attract good faculty and students."
President, West, Public University

"My fundamental educational principles are the ones we talk about all the time: personalized education for every student, an education for a lifetime, including the development of the whole person—quality education. I think you can do a better job in educating in a small context because you can be sensitive to the development—personal and academic—of each student. I think you have to challenge people, whatever their level of ability, to reach that potential—that is our definition of education. Finally, I think an educational institution has to prepare a student for a lifetime of work—different jobs and different careers—and a lifetime of leisure—all of the nonworking hours and days."
President, West, Private College

"The mission of higher education is to provide people with a sound, basic education and not to try to equip people primarily to enter the job market with the most immediately useful tools. Specific knowledge becomes outdated, but basic skills of civilization maintain their validity over time. By well-educated graduates, I mean a person who knows

his native language well, has learned a second language, is at ease with numbers, is able to think and to analyze, and has acquired a value system."
President, East, Private University

" ... strong commitment to academic freedom."
President, West, Public University

Finding a Concept

Fourteen-plus principles, all illustrative. Although they represent repetitive themes in the interviews, it is unlikely that any one of them will fit another person. Most leaders seem to employ a combination of several principles. As stated earlier, the important thing is for leaders to use, to know, and to communicate what those principles are. When questing for the concepts that inform one's own decisions, the following five-step exercise is often helpful.

1. Write down five to ten decisions you have made (new programs, program cuts, hirings, firings, etc.).

2. Determine the common principles or concepts that may have informed those decisions.

3. Write a paragraph elaborating on the principle(s).

4. Quickly list other major and minor decisions that conform to or are an exception to the principle.

5. Think about and list other things that might be done which are consistent with the concept.

Try it. The exercise will probably be useful.

Chapter Three

Implementation Strategies

Less lofty than choosing the "general direction of the college" but equally important for successful leadership is the implementation of ideas. At this stage the focus is on how to get things done, on process and procedures. Concern shifts from Where are we headed? to How do we get there?

Implementation

Throughout academe a remarkable consensus has emerged on the best strategy for implementation. Responses to the general instruction, "Identify and describe administrative principles that tend to be reflected in how you get things done," were item-analyzed and grouped into categories. All concepts mentioned by a majority of the persons interviewed are presented in table 1.

That so few concepts should be mentioned by so many leaders corroborates some basic tenets in successful administration. Loud and clear is the advice that leaders should:

1. Be accessible
2. Be credible
3. Involve more people, earlier.

Each point was made by at least 85 percent of the leaders interviewed. The actual quotations merit study. Rarely do academics reach such consensus. Pervading the quotations on implementation and the general tips that follow is the plea, "Keep your eyes, ears, and mind open." Listen. Involve. Lead.

Table 1: Implementation Strategies

Concept	Percentage Articulating Concept [N = 39]
Be *accessible,* open; walk the campus	89
Be credible, forthright, open, consistent, honest; have a plan	86
Involve more people, earlier; encourage shared *ownership*	86
Initiate: raise issues, float ideas, suggest outcomes	64
Stroke: select good people, back them, praise them, be slow to criticize	64
Decentralize and delegate implementation	64
Keep all constituencies informed, especially trustees	64

Leaders speak on accessibility

"It is important to be visible on campus. This president frequently leaves his office during periods between appointments and goes to the library, visits some faculty offices, and attempts to make appearances at a variety of faculty functions. It is important to meet faculty members on their own ground, in their setting—not always in the president's office."
President, Midwest, Public University

"I try to remain visible by attending student activities, walking the corridors of the classrooms, and meeting with faculty and students over coffee ... every two to three weeks. My wife and I attend many student events."
President, Midwest, Private College

"Keep close to faculty members in informal settings such as the squash court."
President, South, Private University

"I walk a lot on campus. You bump into people, and they see you in places they don't expect to see you. In addition, you see things no one expects you to see. You naturally think about the bigger issues facing the university. I stop and talk to a student and am amazed at what I can learn. If you stay in the office, you are consumed by administrative trivia. Get away."
President, Midwest, Public University

"This president schedules luncheons with all new and transfer students . . . and with each new faculty member. He spends one hour a week minimum wandering around campus, into the classrooms and offices."
President, West, Private College

"I strongly encourage administrators to get out of their offices and onto the campus to meet with faculty members and students—to work with people in their own settings and to be as close to the real meaning and action of higher education as possible."
President, East, Public University

"Stay in touch with what's going on at the university, for example, by attending department meetings, having an open forum where people can ask questions, sending letters to the community, meeting with faculty governance committees. See all incoming mail."
President, Midwest, Public University

"The president has to have a finger on the pulse of the academic life of the institution in order to be a good fund raiser. He must know the institution inside and out . . ."
President, East, Private University

"Knowing the faculty is crucial. That means reading, acknowledging, and displaying faculty publications . . . announced attendance at departmental and college faculty meetings (every several years) . . . convening ad hoc groups of about a dozen faculty members to hear a colleague discuss his or her current scholarship (weekly over breakfast), or to discuss a recent issue of *The Chronicle of Higher Education*, or to listen to a faculty volunteer advancing a new thought on how to run the university . . . arriving early at committee meetings, and stopping to chat en route . . . attending campus cultural events and, occasionally, departmental lectures . . . accepting invitations to end-of-the-term class recitations . . . knowing about and being interested in the activities and the ideas of the faculty."
Vice President for Academic Affairs, Midwest, Public University

"There is a danger in knowing only when things go wrong rather than getting a balanced view.... Walking the campus is important.... Get out on campus every day.... Use faculty luncheons. ... Be accessible to students."
President, East, Public University

"Since there is a danger of not knowing what is going on, the president must insist that staff identify and point out significant problems and events in a timely fashion; that is, 'I don't want any rude surprises.' "
President, East, Private College

"Be alert to signs of divisiveness. Develop early-warning systems.... Recognizing that a faculty does not want to be convinced by its president, find a number of informal mechanisms for exchanging ideas and for determining where pressure points or warning signals are building up on campus."
President, South, Private University

"Retreats with faculty are helpful."
20-year President, Midwest, Private College

"One must learn to listen. Whether or not one agrees with what is said, one must learn to listen and to cultivate the climate in which people will be willing to speak their minds."
President, East, Private College

"Always keep an open mind.... You must let people put forth every idea, no matter how ridiculous.... The idea itself may not be valid, but a derivative of it may be of value. The atmosphere must be conducive to this process."
Vice President for Academic Affairs, East, Public University

"The leader must be willing to listen but should not undermine people who have decision-making responsibilities."
President, Midwest, Public University

"Listening with empathy is crucial. Even turndowns are accepted if the advocate knows he's been heard and senses that I understand the consequences of the decision."
Vice President for Academic Affairs, Midwest, Public University

"Be a careful listener and use tact in taking action. Some institutions have very strong and local constituencies, any one of which could destroy you."
President, East, Private College

"It is important to develop openness with your vice presidents and deans, sharing the bad and the good."
President, Midwest, Public University

"Isolation is one of the worst enemies of the leader. Only your best friend will tell you when you're goofing up. Be sure to have a few close friends."
President, Midwest, Public University

"My style is built on praise and willingness to argue."
President, East, Private College

"I have assembled leaders with academic expertise and management experience to assist me in the university and I do expect them to discuss problems with me. People can disagree in a constructive way and still exhibit loyalty and harmony; once a decision has been made, it is important that administrators down the line support it, even though they may not have personally favored it."
President, South, Public University

"I encourage debate among staff members without permitting rancor to persevere. I encourage argumentation from staff, but once a staff decision is made, I do not permit a staff minority report to go to the board."
President, Midwest, Public University

Leaders speak on credibility

"A president's effectiveness is based on credibility on campus, on a reputation for integrity."
President, Midwest, Private University

"The president must be a 'colleague who is believable,' both in terms of values (the president must personify certain values) and in terms of the role and the function of various groups within the university."
President, East, Public University

"One must be able to change his mind. Humility is a virtue which helps the process. If excessive, it becomes a vice; bending with every gale, wind, or breeze can be harmful."
20-year President, East, Private College

"Above all, personal integrity is a prerequisite for effective administration."
20-year President, Midwest, Private College

"Don't try to work the system; just be certain that the system works."
President, South, Public University

"Fiscal affairs must be credible to the public. This will buy time for more important issues."
President, West, Public University

"Work very closely with the faculty. We don't have to agree at all points, but we must understand each other."
President, West, Private College

Leaders speak on shared involvement

"You can't achieve quality without a shared search for what is best, and that search becomes a vision."
20-year President, Midwest, Private University

"No one person has strength enough to do everything. Always be willing to get help. You must learn to work with people, to establish goals together, and to set common purposes. You must yoke the strength of all together!"
20-year President, Midwest, Private College

"Groups are conservative forces. Part of my problem as president is to pull them away from mediocrity but at the same time to allow them sufficient autonomy so that they will indeed establish their own goals."
President, East, Private College

"You must have a willingness to seek talent and wisdom from other people. An effective leader needs the participation of many people from all parts of the community. You must somehow reach agreement on common goals through participation and communication. This is particularly important in a complex university. . . . Although it is terribly time consuming, it must be done. It is important for people to

be involved and to have participation by faculty and students. That is the keystone of any educational process."
President, Midwest, Public University

"A sense of involvement and shared responsibility is necessary for the success of the programs. This is the most significant of the motivating forces."
President, South, Public University

"In some situations, leadership is subtle. External manifestations of leadership may not be apparent."
Vice President for Academic Affairs, East, Public University

"Leaders are best when they are least overt."
President, East, Private College

"I believe in low-key, low-profile leadership where the leader inserts himself into the situation rather than asserts himself. The ideal is to make everyone feel as if they are reponsible for themselves. 'Unity and autonomy' is the objective of true leadership. The leader builds respect and exercises his authority both wisely and rarely so that it is not weakened."
President, East, Private College

"Where possible make decisions on collective judgment."
President, South, Private College

"Be considerate of other opinions. This sets a tone, a frame of reference, for people."
President, Midwest, Public University

"I think of the classical concept of 'hubris,' or pride. It is the great leveler, for in the classical tradition, pride led to error in judgment—it was the flaw of the classical hero. Today's college president must be ever on guard against too much pride."
President, Midwest, Private College

"A key element in leadership is the avoidance of resentful onlookers."
President, South, Private University

"Be adept at implanting ideas in a person who can 'run with them' through all appropriate channels; use much consultation and accept recommendations; identify opponents in advance, find out why they are opposed, and see if they can be made supporters; try to get

individuals within a group committed before presenting the
recommendation to the whole group."
President, South, Public University

"Bring everyone into the process early enough so that they can feel
involved and can mold the final outcome. Deans, chairmen, faculty
members, students, and others must be treated as if their views are
important, not because of politics but because in fact their views are
important. If people understand why certain decisions are made, the
decisions will be more readily accepted and the sense of fairness will
be enhanced. Use frequent, open meetings, task forces, monthly
newsletters, dinners and evenings, and innumerable individual
conversations to encourage interchange."
Vice President for Academic Affairs, East, Public University

"In the late 1960s the university had changed to a system of
governance that involved equal numbers of students and faculty
members, and by the 1970s the faculty were concerned about this
arrangement.... I strongly encouraged in the faculty an increased
concern for their role and the need for them to take more
responsibility in university governance ..."
President, East, Public University

"Incorporated a feeling of 'participatory democracy' throughout the
university: reorganized ways of doing things so that more people get
involved; opened up better communication—these are the
accomplishments of which I am proudest. Get more people involved in
the business of helping make policy for the university."
Vice President for Academic Affairs, Midwest, Public University

"As times move from expansion to stability, many more people need to
be involved. One must meet regularly and informally with chairmen,
faculty, etc."
Vice President for Academic Affairs, East, Public University

"Give credence to the principles of shared responsibility, authority,
and involvement."
President, South, Public University

"Create an environment for sharing work and for sharing success."
President, West, Public University

"People must be able to participate in the decision-making process and must be able to trust the leadership."
Vice President for Academic Affairs, Midwest, Public University

"The real key to effective leadership is planting ideas and letting them sprout as the ideas of others.... Most academic administrators don't bring the deans, students, and chairs into the decision-making process early enough. One must treat their views as important and give them the sense that they have their input. Involvement is necessary. Note that here open hearings are held on proposed new academic programs."
Vice President for Academic Affairs, East, Public University

"The leader should 'build the decision-making ability of the community.' 'Ability' means involvement of informed individuals in the decision-making process. This means decentralizing the decision authority. It also means introducing a sense of responsibility and a system that facilitates decision making throughout the community.... For example, the academic program evaluation process should emphasize self-study and analysis. Each unit should develop its own ability to analyze and to reflect. This type of process should be institutionalized in order to maintain, insofar as possible, the autonomy of the individual unit."
Vice President for Academic Affairs, Midwest, Public University

"A president's effectiveness often depends on his relationship with the board. The best way to work with the board is to work with the chairman, who is kept informed of everything that happens on campus. I try to deal with each board member in a personal, one-on-one situation at least once a year."
President, Midwest, Private University

"Updated and clarified trustee bylaws contribute to a good relationship with the board. Furthermore, the relationship requires a clear delineation of responsibilities. On a campus, the president has ultimate authority, despite the concept of shared responsibility. With the board, the president must retain the ultimate management role despite the policy-making role of the trustees."
20-year President, Midwest, Private College

"The president must keep the board informed. I use written quarterly reports as well as frequent informal contacts and remember the words of Henry Wriston: 'The board's duty is not to run the college but to see that it is run well.' "
20-year President, East, Private College

"About three years ago I started each August writing an annual statement of goals (about fifteen goals a year) and at the same time reporting on the progress relative to last year's goals. This report is a personally written three- or four-page statement submitted to the board after cooperative development with the staff and colleagues. Goal setting disciplines my thinking and provides general direction to the institution."
Vice President for Academic Affairs, Midwest, Public University

"Send the trustees copies of the student newspaper, the faculty research journal, and development letters. Draft a quarterly presidential newsletter . . . to keep everyone informed of the institution's achievements."
President, South, Private College

"To be effective, the president must maintain communication with the institution's several constituencies in a way that will foster support."
President, East, Private College

"Have a faculty forum where papers are presented, books are reviewed, important issues are discussed."
President, South, Private College

"One of the best things we do with our board is the annual retreat. The members of the board get to know one another personally and they have much more time to work on the college's problems in depth. As a result, they develop a sense of expertise and responsibility for those problems."
President, West, Private College

"Keep people informed about the university. Meet personally with legislators in their home towns, with major newspaper publishers bimonthly. Visit colleague presidents on their campuses. Avoid dissipating time in the officership of national professional associations."
President, West, Public University

"The days of the trusted patriarch are gone into the scrap pile along with the 'old boy' network. Today openness is a prerequisite of trust. Departmental faculty can't be expected to make wise personnel decisions if enrollment projections are concealed."
Vice President for Academic Affairs, Midwest, Public University

"It is important for the administration to give detailed financial analyses to faculty so that they are able to judge whether the administration has budgeted properly."
President, East, Private College

"It is no longer possible to be an S.O.B. or Boss and be president for very long: in today's world, trustees do listen to faculty members and students, and no leader can fool or manipulate them for a long period."
President, South, Public University

"Keeping colleagues thinking they are tuned in on the big picture is essential. So many people believe so often that they are isolated from what is really happening. Each week I spend fifteen minutes rambling about what is going on. This is followed by discussion and comment from my staff. So often they assume that more is happening than is. Also at this weekly meeting I ask them if there is anything I can 'uncork' for the people involved. These sessions are useful, perspective giving, and ego building."
Vice President for Academic Affairs, Midwest, Public University

"Communication with the constituencies of the university is more important than actual involvement with constituencies. A sense of involvement and shared responsibility is necessary for the success of programs."
President, South, Public University

"Candor and openness are essential principles. You must be able to state your objectives to other people."
President, Midwest, Public University

"I consciously neglect routine work to make time to attend and participate in as many academic activities as possible—lectures, plays, discussions, musical events, etc."
President, West, Private College

Leaders list tips

"Avoid as many ad hoc decisions as possible. . . . Regularly seek feedback from associates. . . . Don't be your own secretary. . . . Be prepared to abandon systems and to take on new ones. . . . Delegate considerable authority. . . . Learn how to handle paper quickly; don't let it get in the way of primary responsibilities."
President, Midwest, Public University

"Be tolerant of others. ... Set your own style. ... Encourage other people to come up with ideas. ... Don't let others feel you are giving them orders."
Vice President for Academic Affairs, Midwest, Public University

"Be visible by getting out on campus and by trying not to be out of town too much. ... Don't neglect the faculty. ... Be prompt in answering correspondence. ... Return telephone calls. ... Never have your secretary ask who's calling. ... Remember everything you say or write might show up in the campus newspaper. ... Remember that a good secretary is invaluable. ... Don't neglect the local community. ... Take the initiative and involve others."
President, Midwest, Public University

"Planning time is important. It means an annual work plan and a daily 'to do' list."
Vice President for Academic Affairs, Midwest, Public University

"Use a small book to record thoughts that go through your mind so that you can bring them back when time permits."
President, East, Public University

"Listen. ... Ask who else they have already talked with; ask precisely what they want of you (sympathy, support, decision)."
President, West, Private College

"Form a town-gown council as a mechanism for discussion of broad issues. ... Gain time for reflection by asking appropriate staff to draft letters and speeches. ... Have one or two people who can act as sounding boards on sensitive matters without concern that they might be indiscreet."
President, East, Private College

"Learn from others. ... Know when one can and cannot be precise."
Vice President for Academic Affairs, East, Public University

"Every year have a one-day show-and-tell whereby each dean presents accomplishments and aspirations to the board of trustees."
Vice President for Academic Affairs, Midwest, Public University

"Convince the board of trustees that the college is really theirs by changing the structure of the board, choosing new members, establishing base lines of annual giving for the trustees themselves. This allows the trustees to assume responsibility for the financial

viability of the institution as well as ... the selection, support, or dismissal of management."
President, East, Private College

"Rigidly prescribe search committee procedures."
President, South, Public University

"When newly assuming the presidency, consult widely, announce goals in the inaugural address, and follow with a memo to the community regarding the implementation strategies. The first years are when changes come more easily."
President, East, Public University

"Isolate nine or ten objectives each year. Set them early and mark them off. Do one thing at a time. ... Get up early. ... Handle paper quickly."
President, East, Private University

"If you want to understand the institution, do the budget."
President, South, Private University

"Remember that a president has to live with at least seven publics, each with a strong interest to be nourished."
President, West, Public University

"Listen, then act. It is equally important to act. Letting problems pile up too long can erode confidence. The troops will stay with you most of the time if they believe you are doing something to solve the problems."
President, East, Private College

"A president must be able to remain unthreatened by the inevitable daily crises, and he must be able to be comfortable with the decisions he makes."
President, Midwest, Public University

"Don't lose your temper, don't talk too much, don't be afraid to admit errors, don't get lost in details, don't lose your perspective. Do concentrate on major items among your objectives; do be considerate of everyone and his or her views. Be enthusiastic and objective, be fair, welcome criticism but don't let it get you down. Make sincere efforts to understand the situations that concern others. Work harder than anyone but don't let problems get you down. Above all: relax, be confident, enjoy life, family, and job."
President, West, Private College

"Allocate time to perceive pressure points and note early-warning signals."
President, South, Private University

"Be adept at planting ideas in a person who can 'run with them'. . . . Use consultation . . . accept recommendations. . . . Identify opponents, find out why they are opposed, and see if they can be made supporters. . . . Try to get individuals within a group committed before presenting the recommendation or idea to the whole group. . . . Attend as many student functions as time permits, not overlooking such things as visiting dormitories, the offices of the student newspaper. . . . Exercise honesty in all relations and be credible with all constituents. . . . Don't be surprised if you get sued."
President, South, Public University

"Make learning names a habit. For example, when at a large conference table, have your host make a seating chart for you."
Vice President for Academic Affairs, Midwest, Public University

"Designate former and prospective trustees as fellows and invite them to board meetings and to board committee meetings."
President, East, Private College

"Personal contact is important in solving problems."
Vice President for Academic Affairs, East, Public University

"Invaluable for building public understanding . . . is service in community affairs and on corporate boards. Here I gain access to important information, acquaintanceship with the power structure, an empathy for the business community, and acceptance and understanding for the university."
President, West, Public University

"Define the function of each administrative office, as distinct from the characteristics of the individual holding the office."
President, East, Private College

"Be willing to be respected rather than loved or liked. No good deed goes unpunished."
President, West, Public University

"I think a president going into the job has to give an awful lot of thought to his family. The toll on the spouse and the children is heavy. There is a loss of time and a decline in the quality of time with

them. In addition, children must be helped to learn how to deal with the role so that is doesn't go to their heads. They can be corrupted as much by power as the president can. The spouse and the children also have to be able to deal with the criticisms and the problems that come with the position. I think that is probably the hardest thing for children to handle. The parents can help to control the opportunities for children to abuse the power that goes with the position much more easily and much more readily than they can help the children deal psychologically with the experiences. The children lose their independent identity and, as public figures, are subject to all the dangers that are involved in that—especially the psychological problems. I think this is far more serious than a lot of people realize. I always think of Franklin Roosevelt's children and all they went through. I can see and understand how difficult it must have been for them and their children to live in that context."
President, West, Private College

"Meetings are for reaction. Agendas should start from a recommended solution."
President, East, Community College

"Always acknowledge and respond to correspondence, reports, and phone calls."
President, Midwest, Public University

"Do your homework. Know more."
President, Midwest, Private College

"Never have more than three martinis."
President, Midwest, Public University

"Be prepared."
Vice President for Academic Affairs, South, Public University

"One 'oh, damn' wipes out a thousand 'atta boys.'"
President, East, Private College

"Others perceive that the president has power. The slightest words are often magnified four hundred times. Be careful."
President, South, Private College

"Praise in public; reprimand in private."
President, East, Private College

"Never reorganize; change by increments in less threatening and less ostentatious ways."
President, Midwest, Public University

"Ask for advice only when you will use it."
Vice President for Academic Affairs, West, Public University

"Disagree with an issue, not a person."
Vice President for Academic Affairs, West, Public University

"Operate under a new policy until such and such a date. If no one objects at that date, have all understand that the policy will become permanent."
Vice President for Academic Affairs, Midwest, Private College

"Know the budget."
President, South, Private College

Implementation Overview

The implementation strategy suggested by a synthesis of the preceding advice is shown in figure 1. The leader begins by defining institutional parameters, both educational and ideological. These are the givens, the unchangeables; for example, the institution is funded for public access or tied to a given city. Given the basic parameters, the leader encourages suggestions. The leader listens. Tentative proposals are then advocated by the leader for the sake of provoking further discussion. Discussion is stimulated informally and formally. The original proposal is then revised to reflect these discussions. If the people most affected by the proposal have not yet been involved, they are urged to reformulate and to reshape the proposal into a form they like. The proposal is revised again and a decision is made, usually conforming to a consensus of the recommendations. Then the process of implementation begins.

The president designates an associate to draw up an implementation plan. When approved, implementation is monitored both through the responsible associate and through direct observation (walking the campus). Both the proposal and its implementation are constantly benefiting from additional opinions and experience. Revisions are unending. The leader is always listening and reformulating, even while assuring that action takes place.

THE LEADER . . .

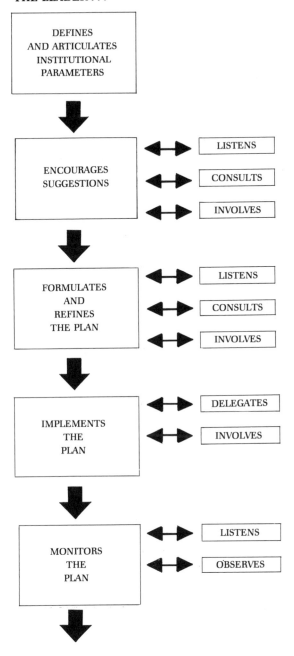

Fig. 1. A basic implementation strategy

Developing New Strategies

The real purpose of studying the preceding quotations is to gain insights on appropriate implementation strategies. Answering the following questions also may help:

1. What routine or new program will get you out on the campus more?

2. Do you know a particularly effective listener? Have you talked with that person about how it's done?

3. Has a routine been established for keeping the board well informed?

4. Can you identify instances when a particular action projected an absence of credibility? to all people or to a subgroup? If so, what might you have done to appear more credible?

5. What tip might you share with a colleague? Why not share it as a means of starting an exchange of tips?

6. Why not check off the quotes that make most sense to you? Why not try them?

Chapter Four

Revitalization Strategies

High and worthy is the leader's challenge to maintain personal vitality, for the challenge we face as leaders is great. Ours is the responsibility not only to keep pace with the times but also to anticipate. Our challenge is to maintain basic institutional momentum, even as the winds of society shift and new technologies arise.

Times change. Many of us were chosen because we promised talents for reconciling student demands and traditional intellectual values, for furthering expansion of faculty and facilities, and for leading institutions whose reliance on even indirect federal funding was miniscule. Those challenges have largely been met and overcome. The challenges ahead are new and different—they always are. In this ever-changing milieu, the leader's imperative is to maintain integrity and effectiveness. For most, remaining effective means constant growth, continuing revitalization. It means constant alertness to new patterns and new circumstances in the society. It means achieving a freshness of perspective.

Such freshness is particularly crucial in colleges and universities. These humane institutions are slow to release stale executives, particularly because these usually single-campus institutions provide few opportunities for horizontal shifts of top executives. Because hierarchy is minimal, so is supervision and coaching. Monies to attend institutes are hard to justify. In higher education, the obligation for revitalization falls less to the institution than to the individual leader.

Revitalization Concepts

The question is how to maintain vitality. The leaders interviewed focused on five learning concepts:

1. *Role models*. Much growth in office stems from self-testing of ideas and techniques observed in the work of respected colleagues. Many presidents are the unrecognized mentors of chief academic officers. Most leaders consciously copy an idea from one colleague, a technique from another. In the school of later learning, our colleagues become our faculty.

2. *Motivation*. A trusted adviser who understands us and our situation is worth a dozen technical experts. Most change or growth occurs because someone who we believe understands our circumstance recommends a decision, not because a technical expert unfamiliar with the institution makes such a recommendation. The growth problem for most of us is not so much ignorance about what to do or to try as it is overcoming a natural aversion to risk.

3. *Access*. Access to role models and to motivators is key. Leaders should build networks of friends and acquaintances who can be called on for advice and who are willing to ask penetrating questions. Access can be increased significantly when a leader becomes an expert in some area of administration or scholarship. An expert who is invited to speak, to consult, or to advise simultaneously has the opportunity to ask, to observe, and to learn. How often have each of us learned more on an accreditation visit than we have given? Is access perhaps a primary reason corporate executives serve on each other's boards?

4. *Routine*. Self-learning is enhanced by habit and intent. "Habit" may be regular attendance at a convention, never missing *The Chronicle*, or annual participation in a week-long workshop. Habit also may be periodically opening conversations with, "What's new lately?" or reading biographies or studying other college catalogs as a hobby. "Intent" is the pursuit of explicit activities that will stimulate self-learning, for example, reflection on how a meeting was conducted or what principles were used in reaching a particular decision at a meeting.

5. *Specifics*. Most growth or change occurs when examples are upon us, when specific failures stare us in the face, for example, when two or three alternatives are judged superior to our current tenure procedures. Specifics goad consideration of alternatives. If the alternatives are adopted, then new principles or general theories need to be found. Then, of course, the new-found theories can lead to a series of deductions and specific actions.

Revitalization Activities

An item analysis of responses reveals that "reading" and "getting away" are the revitalization activities most frequently mentioned: 88 percent mentioned "getting away." (See table 2.)

A special word is needed on reading. The *only* universally read publication in higher education seems to be *The Chronicle of Higher Education:* 83 percent mentioned it. No other publication commands more than 25 percent readership. In the 25 percent category are *Higher Education and National Affairs, AGB Reports, The New York Times,* NASULGC *Green Sheets,* some books on educational administration,

Table 2: Revitalization Strategies

Strategy	Percentage Mentioning Strategy
1. Read, especially *The Chronicle of Higher Education*	88
2. Get away, especially international travel or sabbatical	88
3. Participate in national associations (attendance isn't enough)	69
4. Observe role models, especially former bosses	62
5. Exercise regularly, especially jogging	58
6. Attend workshops and meetings, especially small ones	58
7. Draft major speeches, reports to the board, etc.	50
8. Keep up in scholarly discipline	46
9. Maintain networks among colleague administrators	42
10. Maintain a cultural life and interests beyond the job	42
11. Get involved in projects off campus	35
12. Undergo periodic evaluation	20

some disciplinary journals, and some "life of the mind" magazines (e.g., *Harper's, Scientific American, The American Scholar*). Mentioned by 15 percent were *Educational Record, Liberal Education, Change,* and *Journal of Higher Education.*

About half the persons interviewed expressed a passionate disdain for the literature dealing with higher education administration. The mood is captured in the report on remarks made by the chancellor of the flagship campus of a Midwestern university:

"Sharing not only the titles but also his reasons for selection and the way they affected his thought and leadership style, he first recommended *Working,* by Studs Terkle. It was important because it points out that most people spend their lives in meaningless and unrewarding work, reminding him of his responsibility to make work interesting and satisfying for university employees. Next came *Reality Therapy,* by Robert Glazer, which stresses the need we all have for a sense of self-worth. It reminded him that a university leader must strive to reinforce the self-worth of the faculty and staff of the university. His way was, among other things, to send each employee a personal letter of congratulations for any accomplishment, one that both expressed appreciation for the effort and let the person know the chancellor was familiar with his or her work.

"T. A. Harris's *I'm OK, You're OK* pointed out the need for a university leader to play the adult (mediator) role rather than the parent or the child role when handling personnel problems or conflicts. National Lampoon's *Animal House* brought home the implacability of humor and irreverence in his job. *Theory of Justice,* by John Rawls, which posits the moral justification for the cohesion of society, was a book he regarded highly, so much so that he assigned it to his administrators to read for discussion during their yearly retreat as a means to stimulate in-depth dialogue and thought.

"*Plain Speaking: An Oral Biography of Harry S Truman,* edited by Merle Miller, was mentioned because of his admiration for Truman's ability to make decisions and live with them. Another biography, one on Paul Robeson, alerted him to the barriers that still exist in society and helped to keep him from becoming complacent. *Passages,* by Gail Sheehy, *Cumberland* and *Now and Then,* by Robert Penn Warren; *The Elements of Style,* by Strunk and White; *The Big Gain,* by Gady; *On the Run,* by MacDonald; *Higher Education and the Law,* by Kaplan; and *The Art of Administration,* by Kenneth Eble, completed the list.

"When asked what books he would not recommend, he replied that he rarely read higher education literature."

In sharp contrast, the president of a private college, also in the Midwest, conscientiously reads each new release in the Jossey-Bass series on administration. With the exception of *The Chronicle*, reading patterns are most varied.

Leaders speak on reading

"I read a great deal and discuss what I've read with faculty in relevant disciplines. It is important to understand what is important in contemporary thought."
President, West, Private College

"As a means to pursuing my goal of keeping in touch with life of the mind, I read *The New York Review of Books* and *The New York Times Book Review*. Always I am reading a book, usually biography or some history. Most recently I have been reading the book on MacArthur, *American Caesar*, by William Manchester. Before that I read *Cannibals and Kings: The Origins of Cultures*, by Marvin Harris."
Vice President for Academic Affairs, Midwest, Public University

"The most important thing is the breadth of reading. It matters in an academic community that the president be informed and widely knowledgeable concerning ideas and issues."
President, East, Public University

"A program of reading is, naturally, a personal development strategy. On a regular basis, I read the usual professional journals and studies, *The New York Times, Audubon Society, Smithsonian,* and *National Geographic.*"
President, Midwest, Private College

"My reading of periodicals that relate to personal and professional interests is extensive. I read about thirty nonfiction books a year, especially biographies. Education literature is read when it fits a specific need, but it's generally dull."
President, West, Public University

Leaders speak on getting away

"It is absolutely essential to get off campus ... at least a day and a half a week ... to maintain a broader view of the world."
President, East, Private College

"Get away for one or two nights with the family each month. You move at a different pace in a different setting. . . . You can't be professionally happy without personal happiness. My personal life is the major thing that keeps me going . . ."
President, Midwest, Public University

"Get off campus at least once a month to gain perspective on what's happening on campus."
President, Midwest, Public University

"Much 'rethinking the big picture' is done on trips. I frequently take difficult correspondence in order to mull it over while sitting in a hotel room."
President, Midwest, Public University

"Chairing accreditation teams is a way of getting away and changing pace."
Vice President for Academic Affairs, Midwest, Public University

"One technique to maintain viability, vitality, and vibrancy in the institution and its leaders is the administrative sabbatical—anywhere from six to eight weeks for major administrators. However, lack of administrative depth becomes a problem in small colleges."
President, East, Private College

"Sabbatical leaves for administrators would be highly desirable but are impractical at my university."
President, Midwest, Private University

"I cannot overemphasize the importance of a sabbatical for the long-term president. I was fortunate in having been granted one by my board. A sabbatical provides opportunity for the reflection and revitalization that are fundamental to remaining alive professionally and personally. Moreover, it is almost a necessity that the sabbatical be taken off campus. Unless the president is physically removed, he or she will never really be able to 'get away' from the day-to-day operation of the institution."
20-year President, Midwest, Private College

"I attempt to find times when I can leave my office and go somewhere else in the building to 'hole up' and think. I use travel as a form of brief retreat, using time on planes for both professional and nonprofessional reading and hotel rooms as retreat locations."
President, East, Community College

Leaders speak on meetings and national participation

"I am active in a variety of professional organizations. . . . I derive much . . . from these associations that I utilize to develop administrative concepts and techniques. Like many other college presidents and deans, I occasionally test potential policies and procedures in an off-campus forum. If they pass the scrutiny of peer evaluation, they then may become subject to campus adoption through normal channels and implementation."
20-year President, Midwest, Private College

"My involvement with various national groups is extremely important. . . . this adds a perspective."
President, Midwest, Public University

"Be sufficiently involved in state and national activities (committees, boards, offices) in order to gain new ideas."
President, East, Private College

"Leadership vitality depends on the regeneration that comes from outside jobs: interacting with other presidents . . . serving on a national commission, working on international education, serving on foundation boards or in public policy positions. This puts you in the thick of ideas, reading, discussion of what is new, and forces you to feel the changing circumstances in which you must lead your institution. If you are seen only in work on campus, you are routinized, segmented, dull, and a nervous administrator."
President, Midwest, Private University

"Once you have established a personal relationship with your peers, I believe 'convention going' a virus to be regulated. Higher education is overorganized and meets on the same issues too often. Cultivate junior staff members and read extensively in and outside the profession."
President, West, Public University

"My batteries are recharged by conference attendance."
Vice President for Academic Affairs, Midwest, Public University

"One can learn more from others than from solemn contemplation."
President, East, Private College

"It is very helpful to share ideas, exchange viewpoints. It is helpful to serve as an officer in national, state, and regional organizations as long as one is not overencumbered. It gives one a national posture and a position for viewing national issues. ... You must not get caught in a time trap. Don't catch the disease called 'conventionitis.' You have to decide among meetings, conventions. ... You have to be selective. Develop a system."
President, East, Private College

"We are all subjected to too many unproductive meetings, conferences, conventions, workshops. I greatly restrict my attendance to only a few that are particularly relevant for me at a specific time. Again, my classical background: *quid pro quo*—'something for something.' "
20-year President, Midwest, Private College

"Conferences are generally boring. I go only to meet people I respect and like and to keep those contacts alive."
President, West, Public University

"Frequent get-togethers with other presidents assist one's vitality in at least three ways: by allowing 'gripes to be shared,' by comparing notes on better ways of doing things, and by reinforcing the fact that being president is fun."
President, South, Public University

"I don't gain much from traditional academic meetings, although I do enjoy learning what others are doing in social situations which these meetings engender."
President, Midwest, Public University

"Interaction with colleagues at monthly meetings of the state coordinating board is important."
President, Midwest, Private University

"Probably the most beneficial meeting is an informal group of ten private-college presidents who meet about twice a year and let their hair down. The meetings are not structured and there are no officers. ..."
20-year President, East, Private College

"My best professional meeting is the conference of East Coast Academic Administrators. The smaller meetings are better than larger meetings."
Vice President for Academic Affairs, East, Public University

"I much prefer small meetings to large general meetings."
Vice President for Academic Affairs, Midwest, Public University

"Regular activity in a small group of associations and exchanges of college documents on a regular basis with four or five other presidents are of value."
President, Midwest, Private College

"Go visit another university with eight or nine colleagues for a day or two."
President, Midwest, Public University

Leaders speak on role models

"My mentors were my previous chancellor, also the president and the dean of my alma mater where I subsequently taught. I learned from them a personal leadership style built on praise and a willingness to argue ... to value the liberal arts, bluntness, and the ability and style of being as truthful as I know how to be."
President, East, Private College

"Those whose ideas and concepts have influenced me most over the past several years have been a long-time member of the faculty, a state-coordinating board staffer who is an alumnus of this university, and a private-university president."
President, Midwest, Private University

"Two people have influenced my thinking most over the past several years. The first is a board chairman, a very conservative person; the second is a third-level administrator, a liberal, at this university."
President, Midwest, Public University

"A study of classics provides valuable models of leadership, especially in the broader general context."
President, Midwest, Private College

"I am following in the footsteps of my parents, especially my father (who was a recognized leader of the church), ... serving somewhat out of a sense of obligation, an obligation nurtured by my parents through the words 'you are fortunate and gifted and therefore have great obligations.' "
President, Midwest, Private College

"The person who influenced me most is a Latin teacher who taught me discipline of the mind and how to organize and establish priorities plus a former dean and professor of economics who emphasized the value of thinking critically, analytically, and rationally."
President, South, Private College

"Establish and maintain an active and continuing contact with people on the cutting edge of educational leadership. This refers to persons in various disciplines as well as people in educational administration. It also includes some thinkers of today who are not in education. You need to know the education leaders who are writing and thinking."
President, Midwest, Private College

"Associations with students and faculty are key elements in development."
President, East, Public University

"I learn a tremendous amount about the frontiers of scholarship from interviewing prospective senior faculty, accreditors, consultants. . . . Speakers are reservoirs of knowledge. . . . Quizzing trustees and wealthy friends of the university about their successes often yields helpful insights. It is important to view each encounter as a potential learning experience."
Vice President for Academic Affairs, Midwest, Public University

Leaders speak on exercise, cultural life, and interests beyond the job

Permit one anecdote. At the 1978 ACE annual meeting, thirty-one interviewers were convened to design the question guide. As an aside, these chief executive officers and chief academic officers were asked, "How many are jogging regularly?" Twenty-seven hands went up. One chancellor jogs twenty-five miles a week. This is no normal population.

"Get enough sleep and stay healthy so as not to be irritable."
Vice President for Academic Affairs, Midwest, Public University

"I . . . play handball four times a week."
President, Midwest, Public University

"I . . . wake up with a half hour of rigorous exercises from 3:30 A.M. to 4:00 A.M."
Vice President for Academic Affairs, East, Public University

"I ... regularly exercise in the morning—before breakfast."
President, Midwest, Public University

"I ... jog at least two miles ... at least five days a week."
Vice President for Academic Affairs, East, Public University

"Avoid getting bogged down by the job to the exclusion of other interests."
President, East, Private College

"You should play an active role in organizations outside the one you are directing."
President, Midwest, Private University

"Some type of hobby is important for both physical and mental health."
President, Midwest, Private College

"Get involved in activities outside the university. ... Be exposed to other approaches and opportunities. Live in another world for a time. I have tried to do that by involvement in state activities outside higher education, including some projects and groups in the business community. Involvements in the business world are useful because they provide an opportunity to get caught up in a different environment for a short time. I served on the board of a corporation and had in that connection a relationship with another board member who is also the chairman of the board at a private institution. This has been a very enriching and broadening experience."
President, Midwest, Public University

"I accept only one outside responsibility at a time."
President, East, Private University

Leaders speak on drafting speeches and reports

"Another technique for personal development is the preparation of talks and speeches; such preparations force me to 'continue to be a student,' to try to remain current with my discipline, higher education, and the thinking of those interested in the university."
President, South, Public University

"I don't set aside specific times for thinking about big principles. However, driving is very useful for this purpose and, of course, report writing requires such reflections."
President, East, Private College

"Board meetings and speech writing very often serve the purpose of thinking big principles and charting new directions."
President, East, Private College

"Each year I accept the responsibility for delivering one or two thoughtful speeches. I take time to enunciate a new perspective and make a real contribution."
Vice President for Academic Affairs, Midwest, Public University

"I find myself setting goals through working on university priorities for a fund drive. You can't raise money if you can't articulate the vision of what the university can be, and this shared vision is achieved by developing a shared sense of priorities."
President, Midwest, Private University

"I spend far more time than most of my colleagues at the typewriter actually drafting policy. Most problems are approached by appointing an ad hoc task force. In the charge letter and at the first meeting of this task force I usually identify the problem and suggest a direction to the answer I might take. Such early involvement enables continual interaction with the committee. By disciplining myself to committing ideas to paper, fallacies in logic can be spotted."
Vice President for Academic Affairs, Midwest, Public University

Leaders speak on evaluation

"I believe in periodic evaluation—giving everyone a clear sense of responsibility and then rewarding them for fulfilling that responsibility."
President, East, Private College

"I favor periodic evaluation of presidents and other administrators as a means of maintaining presidential and institutional vitality. At my institution, presidents are periodically evaluated by members of the administration, and those reports are sent to the board."
President, Midwest, Private University

"Engage in regular self-study and evaluation."
President, Midwest, Private College

Leaders speak on keeping up in the discipline

"The most important thing is to stay alive in one's profession. . . . One never has to 'compromise a decision,' because one can always return to the profession . . ."
Vice President for Academic Affairs, East, Public University

"I teach freshmen and run the lab . . . am very close to the discipline. I regard staying alive in my field as the crucial mechanism for maintaining vitality. . . . Many presidents have commented on the contribution their academic discipline has made to their presidency. They have almost invariably cited the value of the technique used to organize material in making neutral decisions. For example, I regularly draw upon the scientific method, intellectual curiosity, and the value of organized and disciplined appraisal. . . . I firmly believe that stubborn insistence upon staying vital in my own academic discipline has not only made me a far more successful chief executive but also provided an atmosphere where I can look forward to returning to a faculty post rather than fear departure from the presidential office."
President, South, Private University

"I think it important for an administrator to keep involved in normal academic activity such as teaching and research."
President, Midwest, Public University

"Until about two years ago I continued to teach. However, I gave it up because too many classes were being missed and I couldn't keep up to date. It would take me up to two years to get back in shape in the discipline."
President, East, Private College

"I thought it was possible for the president to maintain an active role in teaching a science course. I came to realize that in doing so I was serving my own interest instead of keeping in touch and remaining vital. The ad hoc demands on a president's time make it impossible to maintain the regularity necessary to perform the job of teaching with quality."
President, South, Public University

Leaders speak on length of an effective presidency

One revitalizing option is to change jobs, a not uncommon strategy. That raises the inevitable question, For how long is a president effective? Here, three themes emerged: (1) it depends on the individual and the situation; (2) most presidents accumulate enemies and make only temporary friends; and (3) about four to ten years, typically.

"The length of a presidency depends on the individual and the circumstances. The day it is no longer any fun, the president should get out."
President, East, Private College

"There is no quantitative limit on how long the president can be effective. As long as a person is able to maintain a freshness of view and vitality and doesn't feel jaded he can be successful."
20-year President, East, Private College

"As long as they perceive that there is a challenge to be met, they can be effective."
Vice President for Academic Affairs, East, Public University

"How long a president is effective depends on time, place, and circumstances."
President, Midwest, Public University

"The presidency is a temporary position that some of us occupy longer than others based on how long it takes us to create a coalition of opposing factions. The implication here is that the more change a president is responsible for, the shorter his term may be, unless he is able to be a very astute politician, and even then his days are numbered."
President, East, Private College

"There is no specific number of years during which a college or university president can be effective, but in order to be effective the president probably needs a minimum of four years. ... It might be difficult to maintain effectiveness beyond the eighth or ninth year of a presidency."
President, Midwest, Public University

"I have been here too long. Institutions, like people, need new faces, fresh ideas, and enthusiasm in their leadership positions."
20-year President, West, Public University

"Effective leadership requires a long-term commitment to an institution. ... too many individuals accept the presidency with the

intention of using it as a stepping-stone. . . . a truly effective administrator establishes himself over a long period of time. Furthermore, he really is not fully accepted until the institution has weathered some bad times under his leadership."
20-year President, Midwest, Private College

A chief executive officer is effective:

". . . roughly ten years."
President, South, Private University

". . . four to ten years."
President, Midwest, Private University

". . . five to ten years."
Vice President for Academic Affairs, East, Public University

". . . about ten years."
President, South, Public University

". . . a self-imposed ten years."
President, West, Private College

Questions to Contemplate

1. Is it time to resign or change jobs?

2. When do you think "big principles"? When you are drafting speeches? When you are attending conferences? When you are driving? When you are alone?

3. What specific developmental activities do you intend to undertake during the next three years? What needs do you have? What opportunities are there?

4. What more can you do to urge or to enable your associates to maintain vitality?

Chapter Five

Leadership Profiles

Another way to rethink leadership strategies is to study a list of skills that presidents and chief academic officers think they most need in their jobs. In turn, personal strengths and weaknesses can be self-assessed and a self-development strategy designed.

Leadership Hypotheses

Three "umbrella" characteristics were identified from a long list of hypotheses solicited from the interviewers at the beginning of the project (see Appendix B). A leader must (1) provide a *sense of direction*, (2) project a *sense of enthusiasm*, and (3) furnish a *structure for implementation*. All three sets of skills are essential for success.

The leader with a sense of direction

- *Thinks future possibilities.* The leader relates decisions to a sense of where the college is headed, what it might be ten years from now (e.g., college will become a major research university, college will become a center for adult, part-time learning, private college will become public).
- *Recognizes present momentum.* The leader relates decisions to the historic strengths of the college, to the convictions of those who populate the institution, to a realistic assessment of the current circumstances (educational, fiscal, geographic), to a sense of where the college has been (e.g., college was a normal school, university has been strong in plastics research for three decades, biological science departments are proudly separate).

- *Holds educational convictions.* The leader relates decisions to three or four general principles about how students learn, what roles are appropriate for colleges, what kinds of knowledge should be part of every curriculum, or how faculty relates to the college mission (e.g., students learn best in a trust-filled setting, colleges make learning resources more readily available, academic freedom is essential to the critical process).

- *Thinks globally.* The leader analyzes decisions by thinking bigger— longer terms, higher principles, broader categories, wider geography (e.g., implications of precedent setting are considered, cost of maintenance is added to cost of purchase, larger risks are taken, effect of local decision on the environment is queried, recommended solution is compared with solution in another culture).

- *Relates personal values.* The leader relates decisions to a personal respect for all mankind, a conviction that people are more important than procedures (e.g., honesty, regard for all people, people have a right to know).

The leader with a sense of enthusiasm

- *Thinks positively.* The leader demonstrates great self-respect, discerns the best in everyone and every circumstance, redirects thinking from problems to challenges, builds self-respect in others.

- *Acts with energy.* The leader is an exemplar of commitment, drive, enthusiasm.

- *Possesses interpersonal skills.* The leader motivates others, nurtures self-respect in associates, uses humor effectively, empathizes with associates, projects charisma.

The leader who provides a structure for implementation

- *Respects expertise in others.* The leader listens, consults, delegates, recognizes self-limits, decentralizes, works effectively through others.

- *Recognizes right time and place.* The leader alters methods and assigns weights to concerns after assessing the particular situation, worries about good timing, decides promptly unless there are reasons to delay, and understands the context of decisions.

- *Understands campus ethos.* The leader minimizes faux pas by recognizing the distinctive decentralized authority structure of colleges, knowing that leading is with the consent of the governed, understanding the informal power structure, sensing the difference between managing a business and administering a college.
- *Implements by increments.* The leader breaks tasks into achievable steps, bounces back from temporary setbacks, appreciates that slow change is progress, relishes partial successes, avoids ultimatums, avoids becoming dogmatically wed to one way, encourages and praises alternative and even contradictory approaches, demonstrates relentless patience.

Among essential talents, the most crucial is the capacity to provide a sense of direction. Direction, vision, integrity, coherence are distinctive responsibilities of the leader. The leader's highest mission and most essential talent is to know, to shape, and to articulate what the college or university is becoming.

Leaders Speak

The primacy of sense of direction is revealed by how leaders interviewed distributed 100 "weighting points" among the three categories (see Question 10, Appendix A). As shown in table 3, 54 percent assigned the highest number of points to sense of direction.

Table 3: Percentage Weighting Leadership Characteristic Most Heavily

Category	Sense of Direction	Sense of Enthusiasm	Implementation Sense
All leaders interviewed	54	26	20
Presidents only (excludes CAO's)	53	31	16
Chief academic officers only (excludes CEO's)	56	17	28
Leaders from private institutions	43	40	17
Leaders from public institutions	62	14	23

Typically, sense of direction received 40 points; sense of enthusiasm, 31; and implementation sense, 29. Leaders in public institutions stressed sense of direction even more than private institution leaders (see table 3).

The biggest difference, however, was in the importance placed on sense of enthusiasm by private college leaders (most important for 40 percent) versus public college leaders (most important for only 14 percent). Among private institutions, the structure of implementation is either more obvious, or the need for an enthusiastic president is greater, or both. Here, and throughout the interviews, the lesson is that different institutions and different times require different skills and different strategies. There is no single prototype of an effective leader.

Whatever the style, a sense of direction is crucial. It is a universal requirement for leadership. The leader's sense of direction grows from imagining future possibilities, grounding plans in historical reality, and applying a consistent set of educational convictions. Personal values are subordinate to more generally held educational convictions about where the college is and should be headed. The context is more local and immediate than global and long term. The sense of direction is an optimistic view of the possible, not normally a dream. Responses within each category are shown in table 4. The necessity for interpersonal skills and of respecting expertise in others is also evident.

Enthusiasm gains meaning when it inspires others. Lonely on top it is, but the top cannot do it alone. Hard work and optimism must be contagious if the leader is to succeed. The leader must draw out others, must capture their imagination and expertise. The go-it-alone leader is probably going down. Our lesson is to develop and use interpersonal skills and to listen to the experts around us. Ironically, leaders who listen have more say.

Finally, our profiled leader must have the *capacity to decide.* The chair of a meeting must rule a motion either in or out of order if the meeting is to proceed; so also a leader must provide guidelines by saying yes and no. Decisions must be timely, well informed, just, and appropriate—most of all there must *be* decisions. This final attribute wins its place among the original twelve by write in, as in a write-in candidate on a ballot. Perhaps the interviewers took this characteristic for granted and therefore did not mention it in the hypotheses suggested. In any case, it was omitted.

The omission was discovered in two ways. First, a panel of experts on leadership, drawn from government, industry, and academe, was

Table 4: Percentage Identifying Subcategories As Most Important

Sense of Direction

Thinks future possibilities	34
Recognizes present momentum	25
Holds education convictions	27
Thinks globally	4
Relates personal values	10
Total	100

Sense of Enthusiasm

Thinks positively	29
Acts with energy	18
Possesses interpersonal skills	53
Total	100

Implementation Sense

Respects expertise in others	56
Recognizes right time and place	23
Understands campus ethos	13
Implements by increments	8
Total	100

Source: Question 10, National Interviews plus Conference Interviews. Based on 49 interviews.

Note: Comparisons of percentages *between* subcategories (e.g., "Thinks positively" with "Recognizes present momentum") should not be made, because each group has a different number of subcategories.

asked to extend the list. All three panelists mentioned "the capacity to decide" as the missing element. Second, the chief executive officers and the chief academic officers attending the Leadership Vitality Conference were asked to "identify the characteristic that is missing"; two-thirds mentioned "willingness to decide" or "decisiveness" or "making concrete decisions." Clearly, the capacity to decide should be part of the leadership profile.

Our profile is now complete. The prototypical chief executive officer or chief academic officer owns a vision, a vision shaped by history, by expert advice, and by educational conviction. Through an enthusiastic belief in the vision, the leader inspires others to work toward it. The leader's special role is to conceptualize a sense of direction, to inspire others to pursue it, and to set explicitly the boundaries and the strategies of the pursuit.

Leaders speak about a sense of direction

"A leader must be able to predict problem areas and the forces of the winds of change. ... It is like steering a ship and keeping it on course ..."
President, Midwest, Public University

"The most important thing in remaining vital as a leader is to view the institution as an organic, developing, growing, changing thing. A leader must always have vision into the future so that he or she is able to maintain a sense of excitement about what the institution can become."
President, East, Community College

"The first thing that makes for effective leadership is that the person has to have a vision about the future. The person has to be able to think, not merely about day-to-day activities and efforts, but about ten years from now, and have in mind some idea of what he wishes to accomplish and what he wants the institution to be doing at that point in the future."
President, West, Private College

"Assess carefully the room for constructive change. Although you must lead, you cannot get too far ahead of the members of the community if you are to have their support."
President, East, Private College

"Understand the institution as a basis for reasoned judgment."
President, West, Public University

"Leadership in a college is recognizing opportunities, understanding the idiosyncratic. It is really the result of incremental decision making. You don't declare a new frontier or a new foundation. ... Actually, you can only accelerate or retard an evolution. There are very few

revolutionary changes at a college. . . . You lead by your ability to
recognize an alternative is needed and by seeing an opportunity."
President, Midwest, Private College

"The president is wise enough not to ask for a vote until secure on the
outcome and brave enough to say that if he is more than convinced
that he is right, he will overrule the poor decision and take
responsibility for the consequences."
President, South, Private College

"To be an effective leader the president must believe in the kind of
institution that she or he is administering."
President, East, Private College

"I believe a close coordination exists between institutional direction
and personal aspiration."
President, Midwest, Private College

"You must have clearly thought out values of your own so as to make
your behavior predictable."
President, Midwest, Public University

Leaders speak about a sense of enthusiasm

"To be a leader, a sense of 'well-ness'—physical, mental, emotional,
and spiritual— is absolutely necessary."
President, South, Public University

"The leader needs a strong ego, needs to be assertive, with an urge
and need to succeed, and must like people."
President, Midwest, Public University

"I believe strongly in the willingness and ability of people to make
accommodations, to recognize the universities as diverse communities,
and to uphold respect for diversity and individual values. 'Humanity
may be reclaimed.' I am fundamentally optimistic!"
President, East, Public University

"A person needs a tremendous amount of energy and willingness to
work in order to be an effective leader."
President, Midwest, Public University

"A leader enjoys being involved with persons who are thinking and doing. The leader's enthusiasm helps to reinforce the enthusiasm already there."
Vice President for Academic Affairs, East, Public University

Leaders speak about an implementation sense

"The most important task of a president is to appoint outstanding VP's."
President, West, Public University

"It's important to hire good people and then let them do the job assigned in their own way. I would sacrifice managerial abilities for the ability to attract brilliant people."
President, West, Public University

"By capitalizing on the strength of others, I enhance my own leadership vitality."
President, Midwest, Private College

"What has worked once should not mislead you into thinking that it will work again. Be prepared to abandon systems and to take on new ones."
President, Midwest, Public University

"The nature of leadership depends on personal style and on the situation."
Vice President for Academic Affairs, East, Public University

"A president must have a sense for the *academic* community. Decisions in universities really are made differently from those in the business world."
President, Midwest, Public University

"The crucial ability for an effective leader is the understanding of the campus ethos, mood, proper timing. Bypassing the normal aculturation that occurs as an individual passes through teaching, the department chairship, and the deanship is extremely hazardous."
Vice President for Academic Affairs, President, Public University

"A leader must not be too far in front or too far behind those he is leading. When the leader is too far out of step, those being led will be

marching each to a different drummer; or the leader will be led instead of providing leadership."
President, South, Private College

"Effective leadership means that one must be different in different times. The late 1960s was a period of crisis management, where there was no time for tranquil contemplation. Since then the period has been one of thoughtful and continual vigilance."
President, East, Private College

"Effective leadership will vary according to the environment and the expectations."
President, Midwest, Public University

"The effectiveness of a leadership style varies with the situation. Multiple styles are effective. The impact will vary depending on the context and the actors."
Vice President for Academic Affairs, Midwest, Public University

Leaders speak about the capacity to decide

"It is ... important to act. Letting problems pile up too long can erode confidence. The troops will stay with you most of the time as long as they believe you are doing something to solve the problem."
President, South, Private College

"The key to a successful presidency does not lie in the number of good decisions which are made so much as in the avoidance of bad decisions."
President, Midwest, Public University

"With the approaching budget and enrollment crunch, I have tended to become more assertive. I am more comfortable and confident in making decisions. The environment we are in requires more decisions."
President, Midwest, Public University

"The balance between a willingness to look forward and a need to remain sensitive is crucial. I have seen so many people who allow power to go to their heads and who become insensitive to others. I have also seen a number of people destroyed because they are too sensitive and lose their capability for leadership because they can't deal with criticism."
President, West, Private College

Leaders Portray Leaders

The crazy quilt of skills takes form in an individual—a leader—who often hasn't thought about the skills separately. To catch a sense of what leaders are and can be, read the leadership profiles that follow. Each profile was written by an interviewer about a person interviewed. Names and places have been changed to preserve anonymity.

Profile one

"One must be truly impressed by the personal and professional stamina of anyone who has spent almost a quarter of a century in college administration. For the past twenty-one years, Dr. Classic has been president of a college. Prior to assuming this position, he was a vice president and dean of the graduate school at a state university. Hence, his administative career has spanned the major challenges of modern higher education—the age of expansion, the period of campus unrest, and now the uncertainty of steady state or declining enrollment.

"The pattern and timetable of Dr. Classic's career indicate that he is not the product of graduate programs in higher education. Like many of his colleagues in the independent sector of higher education, he is from the ranks of a traditional academic discipline—in his case, the classics—a fact that does not take long to discern.

"Dr. Classic's conversation is punctuated with historical and literary allusions that betray classical influences. In addition, he is an articulate spokesman for the liberal arts, a spokesman whose sincerity reveals more than simply a vested defense of his type of institution. During the interview, Dr. Classic credited his academic training with providing him the personal discipline that has been so essential in maintaining his professional perspective throughout the years of shifting challenges.

"All of this is not to say, however, that Dr. Classic is a contemporary Mr. Chips—philosophically astute but pragmatically ineffectual. He is as much at home in a corporate board room as he is discussing *The Republic* with faculty colleagues. During his presidency, he has been successful in providing not only the academic leadership for a major curriculum revision but also the developmental expertise necessary to raise more than $25 million for the advancement of his college.

"Dr. Classic has been, and is, quite active in a variety of professional organizations. He appears to derive much of his leadership vitality from these associations, which he utilizes to develop administrative concepts and techniques. Like many other college presidents and deans, Dr. Classic occasionally tests potential policies and procedures in an off-campus forum. If they pass the scrutiny of peer evaluation, they may then be adapted for campus use through the college's normal channels of implementation.

"'Normal channels' is significant. While Dr. Classic likes to credit the survival of his lengthy and successful presidency in part to his mastery of the talent to lead through example, he also relies on other college leaders to coordinate those politically sensitive efforts necessary to achieve the institutional cooperation so essential to campuswide acceptance of innovative policies and programs. As Dr. Classic observes, 'administration is the art of getting things done through other people.' More bluntly stated, a college president must, according to Dr. Classic, delegate authority with responsibility or 'go to the funeral home.'

"Consequently, Dr. Classic is impressive in his pragmatic approach to college administration. By capitalizing on the strength of others, he enhances his own leadership vitality."

Profile two

"'The nature of the personality determines the leadership style. My own leadership style carries with it a desire to work with groups of people to achieve objectives. The nature of my personality is such that I work to influence others to move toward goals. There is no need for personal aggrandizement; the leader should not be self-centered; true leadership must have a selflessness in it.' These words, spoken by the president of a progressive liberal arts college for women, reflect the ethos of the college. Responsibility is delegated by the president to individual members of the staff and to teams of faculty, staff, and students. The president acts on her belief that a high level of trust between persons and groups that work together is necessary in order to maximize the use of each person's time and effort. Recognition that most problems are best solved by a team approach is, in her opinion, in the best interests of the institution and is in direct opposition to personal aggrandizement.

"Underlying her ability and inclination to delegate responsibility is a deep respect for expertise in others and a recognition that the collective wisdom of a well-selected group is often greater than that of an individual. The president's role, in her view, is to help on the periphery, planting ideas and nurturing them as they develop. She counsels that a president should avoid preempting the responsibility of another administrator (or of a team), even if she knows she can do it better than the individual (or team) to whom the assignment is given. Even when things may not be as well done, there may be other benefits derived from delegating that responsibility. A primary benefit can be the building of trust between colleagues. When decisions are made, she believes that it is crucial for the president to back up the staff or group, even when she may not be in total agreement with the action taken. The president who fails to underpin the staff or team destroys the trust that unites them for effective action. Although the president who delegates is vulnerable to criticism for the action of others, the reality is that, at best, the president can only orchestrate the instituition; she cannot run it in detail.

" 'Effective leadership carries with it knowledge of where one is going. It is important that colleagues think in a similar, but not identical, vein; a certain amount of disagreement is necessary to crystallize thoughts.' Planning for the future in a comprehensive, institutionwide approach, involving faculty, staff, students, trustees, and alumnae, is a priority for this president. She predicts that within the next three to four years the college will be widely recognized in the curricular area—design of programs—for its imagination, creativity, and responsiveness to changes in society. The college will continue to engage in substantive curricular planning, focusing on the fact that it is a women's college with a unique obligation to identify and offer programs to prepare women for emerging career fields. She expects the college to concentrate on goal setting in planning and with students. She looks forward to removing sexual, racial, and other biases from the curriculum in a collegewide effort not yet achieved in other institutions.

"Believing that there need be no forced choice between a liberal and a specialized education, this president emphasizes the fundamental importance of liberal studies that inform everything one does. She believes with conviction that there is no magic formula for structuring a liberal education program. She supports the college's effort to reexamine its approach to providing a liberal education. She feels that to be liberally educated one must be conscious of the humanity of others, of one's heritage, of different cultures. A liberal education should be designed to emphasize the importance of seeking one's personal goals and of providing adequate skills to reach those goals. She believes that a liberal education must be designed to prepare one for the most significant phenomenon of contemporary life: change.

"This president points out that every president acts in a context and that her present context is in a dynamic and responsive college which has identified and appreciated her flexibility in not imposing a model on the institution that is inappropriate to its traditions or potential."

Profile three

" 'My principal charge as president is to make decisions for this institution. It is better to make decisions in a timely manner than to feel that every decision must be right and thereby delay in reaching decisions. This institution could not function if I always waited to be *sure* that I was making the right decision.'

"The president of this comprehensive research university places great emphasis on being as familiar as humanly possible with the details of every situation. He feels strongly that his credibility as president is tied to a profound and evident knowledge of the institution. This understanding helps him appreciate the problems that his colleagues are addressing and is valuable to him as the university's principal fund raiser. Although he strives to know the details of situations, the actual management is left to others in whom he has confidence. He admits that in his effort to learn the details of the institution, he has enormous difficulties in managing his time; but for the sake of his own time and energy he would not wish to emulate presidents who have delegated so much authority that they have almost lost touch with the inner workings of the institution they were attempting to lead.

"In making decisions, he does not rely heavily on a systems approach, but he does want data and likes to see alternatives. Although he does consider factors such as cost effectiveness, he believes that most of his decisions are more intuitive than systematic. He feels that he must be continuously on guard to prevent the *urgent* from driving out the *important*. He keeps on his desk a quotation from A. Lawrence Lowell which asserts that a university president should never feel hurried, because working under pressure interferes with the serenity of judgment needed for making major decisions.

"In order to deal with a broad range of responsibilities, he has become adept at 'compartmentalizing' his activities. He has developed a capacity to switch dramatically from one thing to another and to give all of his attention to one thing at a time so that his thoughts are almost never divided. He does not internalize the institution's problems. He describes his situation as having been assigned a long-term part to play as president. He admits that he likes the role and enjoys playing the part, but knows full well that the part is not the person.

"'It is not right for the president of an institution to be the chief architect of the curriculum,' he asserts. Therefore, although he expresses his ideas about higher education freely in speeches and in publications, he does not link them to his institution.

"In order to avoid a feeling of *déjà vu* as his presidency matured, he chose to involve himself in other intellectual activities, such as writing for *The London Times* and *Daedalus* and serving on corporate boards. Although these activities bring variety to his life, they cause him to be desperately overloaded.

"In reflecting on effective leadership in higher education, he suggests that in a large, comprehensive university the key is the ability to manage an extraordinarily complex budget. In regard to budget management, three things are true: (1) If one assumes the presidency of such an institution without experience in managing big budgets, one may be in serious trouble from which there is no way to recover; (2) one can manage a complex budget *well* only after considerable experience; and (3) one has to have a special gift to manage budgets of this nature well—this kind of budget management is not a science, but an art."

Profile four

"Wryly, with a barely perceptible twinkle in his burnt-umber eyes, Dr. C. explained the most important experiences that had prepared him to be the chief academic officer of a medium-sized land-grant university in the East: 'As a bartender I met all kinds of people and learned how to deal with them; as a jazz musician I learned how to get along without much sleep.'

"Indeed, broad-scope communication and a sleep-shy daily schedule do appear to be two hallmarks of his administrative style.

"A biological scientist who had served for a decade as department head and for a year as college dean at a large Midwestern university, Dr. C. was selected in 1972 to be the chief academic officer of an institution intent on transforming a good four-year institution with few graduate programs into a comprehensive university. Times were hard: student unrest, increasing government involvement, decreased public confidence, financial duress, and an early move toward faculty collective bargaining.

"Now, more than six years later, Dr. C. can reminisce and speculate on the methods that allowed him to weather the storms and sail successfully along the charted course. He advises:

- Plant seeds and water them so that when they sprout the idea is viewed as that of others.
- Decentralize. If it doesn't work, change the people.
- Insist on objectives and priorities. Avoid funding until people get their act together.
- Assess strengths and weaknesses and plan accordingly, using budgets as key elements in the planning structure.
- Stay active professionally so that you never have to compromise a decision but can always return to teaching and research.
- Keep up with national developments in higher education through reading and especially direct discussion.

"Broad and intense communication is another hallmark of Dr. C.'s style. Bring everyone into the process early enough so that they can feel involved and can mold the final outcome. Deans, chairmen, faculty, students, and others must be treated as if their views are important, not because of politics but because, in fact, their views *are* important. If people understand why certain decisions are made, the decisions will be more readily accepted and the sense of fairness will be enhanced. Dr. C. uses frequent open hearings, task forces, monthly newsletters, dinners and evening meetings, and innumerable individual conversations to encourage free interchange.

"A powerful life force harnessed to a Spartan discipline creates time for communication and for the richly varied activities that make up successful leadership. Dr. C. rises at 3:15 A.M., works pulleys and wheels for an hour, dresses and breakfasts, and then begins his working day with an hour's reflection in his still-quiet household. Office work begins at 6:30 A.M., a quiet time that proves to be unusually productive. When the administrative team is complete at 8:30 A.M., Dr. C. has a three-hour head of steam for energizing any who need to feel its live heat. After a full day of the usual administrative turmoil, the time between 5:00 and 6:00 P.M. is often devoted to winding down, to a bantering exchange with office colleagues before returning home. Saturday and Sunday hours in the office are not unusual.

"Dr. C. enjoys a self-confidence derived from the knowledge that he is on top of his job, aware of all he should be, and equipped by dint of experience and hard work to meet each challenge. Invited to become a candidate for a presidency more than once, he prefers his present role as an inside man. He believes a chief academic officer can reach a peak in the fifth or sixth year and can maintain that for another five to six years. An officer who is building an institution can be effective for as long as twenty or twenty-five years. Given Dr. C.'s discipline and his capacity for renewal through communication, he probably can."

Profile five

"The most interesting characteristic of William Strength's presidency is his independence. He believes the president must be insulated from the current operations of the university in order to have an overview of objectives and needs that is unobscured by daily crises. To do this, the president must surround himself with associates who are willing and able to assume full responsibility for their assigned duties. He keeps informed by regular weekly meetings with these associates, both individually and as a group, but does not allow them to shift decision making to him.

"In both his private and his professional lives, Strength operates by a set of precepts that preserve his independence. Several examples will serve to illustrate this:

- Social engagements are declined if they require being away from home more than two evenings in a row, and none are accepted for Sunday evenings.
- Appointments are not made for anyone unwilling to disclose the topic and purpose of the requested meeting.
- Meetings with organized groups must be arranged so that neither the university nor the president appears to sanction the organization.
- All paperwork is assigned to someone other than the president unless it is marked personal. If presidential action is required, Strength requires a recommendation for his consideration, but will not originate one.
- The president is satisfied to be respected. He is unconcerned about being liked or loved.
- The president takes five weeks' leave each summer and 'cannot imagine circumstances' at the university which would induce him to cut that time short.

"President Strength has developed a catechism for testing all decisions. His ability to apply this catechism requires information, objectivity, and analytical power, all of which are enhanced to the extent he is successful in his demand for independence. The principal elements of the catechism are as follows:

- Will the proposed action enhance the freedom of the university from political interference?
- Will the proposed action improve standards?
- Will the proposed action enhance the ability of the university to attract good faculty and students?
- Is the proposed action timely?
- Is the proposed action politically feasible?"

Profile six

"President Wonder learned early on that he 'cannot do everything, and not even everything important,' with the result that he sometimes neglects routine work to do those things he believes contribute most significantly to leading his college. For him, the most important ingredient in leadership is credibility, and he devotes the greatest part of his time and energy to activities that strengthen his credibility:

- Extremely broad consultation on new appointments, e.g., President Wonder met separately with more than two-thirds of the faculty members before appointing the recommended candidate to the position of Dean of the Faculty.
- Attendance at, and participation in, as many campus activities—lectures, plays, recitals, etc.—as possible.
- Extensive reading within the disciplines available at the college, followed by discussions with individual faculty members and departments about the intellectual content and development of those disciplines.
- Accessibility of the president to listen and discuss all promotion and tenure recommendations before making final decisions.
- Active and wide consultation with members of the faculty on all decisions within the college.
- Continuous consultation with members of the board so they will be fully informed and aware of the educational consequences of actions they take.

"In all of these activities, President Wonder's objective is to ensure that members of the college community understand the reasons for decisions and actions he takes. President Wonder is not seeking consensus, because he believes the college would not move forward if that were required."

Profile seven

"When this president assumed office some years ago, he became the leader of an institution that was poor in all respects: finances, quality, enrollment, faculty, and facilities. The primary goal he set was to enhance quality. The president recognized that, because the institution was poor financially, little could be accomplished without additional resources, so much of his time was devoted to that effort. At the same time, he knew that the institution could not develop if the old administrative style was maintained. The popular leadership style at that time was of a fatherly type, with little faculty involvement in governance; decisions came directly from the president's office. He deliberately set out to set up a structure to bring about faculty involvement in governance and brought in a group of administrators to whom he delegated authority and responsibility.

"Through hard work, he has established a national reputation as an education leader and has served as an officer in many national, state, and regional organizations. He is an effective fund raiser. As a result the campus has grown in size and beauty. The percentage of faculty with Ph.D.'s has more than doubled. The quality of students has not improved as much at the matriculating as at the graduating end. He has succeeded remarkably well in moving toward his goals, but improvement in quality remains his chief goal.

"He is deeply loved on campus and is respected in the community. He has a deep love for his institution, a love so strong that he has rejected offers from institutions that paid more and had fewer problems. At the same time, he has the ability to appraise himself and his institution objectively. Although he has been in office for a long time, he works just as hard today as he ever did. Many goals have been achieved, but he continues to work diligently, to help the institution raise its sights and accomplish new goals.

"He has not succeeded in all his goals on the first try, but he has not given up when he failed. He is strong-willed and strong-minded, but, when wrong, he has been willing to change directions or approaches.

"He credits much of the institution's progress to others. He does delegate responsiblity and authority, and the team of people working with him recognize that they are important contributors. He remains something of a father figure, but of a modern family in which the father doesn't make all the decisions but shares the chores and many important decisions with the family.

"He is an example of a person who has found a place where he can succeed and has been happy with the success."

Profile eight

"President Energetic knows more about the operating details of his university than any other president I know. His knowledge is encyclopedic and is equaled by his understanding of why things work as they do and how to change them if necessary. This results partly from the president's tremendous energy and partly from his belief about how to stay alive managerially. It is reported that he has been seen at sports events reading computer printouts of detailed operating information on various organizational elements of the university, devoting the same interest and intensity other fans devote to their programs and the game itself. He has the ability, months later, to cite specific information from these printouts accurately and to use it analytically in making decisions.

"More important, President Energetic believes he should manage two or three organizational units at all times and that he should be responsible for these units for periods of two or three years. He selects as candidates units that need a change in leadership, that have problems he finds interesting, or that would contribute to balanced workloads for his key subordinates. By deliberately changing the composition of his work, President Energetic believes that the presidency could continue to be interesting indefinitely and that he will be less likely to stagnate and become ineffective. Otherwise, he believes, a president is unlikely to contribute much to a university after five years in office."

Questions to Contemplate

1. What do you think is the important point in this chapter? Does this point suggest that you should alter your present behavior, e.g., allocation of time? If so, how?

2. Write *capacity to decide* at the bottom of Question 10, Appendix A. Check the several characteristics you think are most important in your present situation. Put either an "S" (one of your strengths) or a "C" (concerns, maybe weaknesses) by each of the thirteen characteristics. Star the characteristic that your spouse (or close associate) would regard as your greatest strength. Look over the results. Does this exercise suggest that you should alter your present behavior? If so, how?

3. Should a fourteenth item be added to the list? If so, what? (Drop me a note.)

4. What are the strengths and weaknesses of your associates? Compare them with your own. Do your associates' strengths compensate for your concerns or weaknesses? How should you be working with your associates?

Chapter Six

Professional Renewal Strategies

When a trained economist or historian or microbiologist shifts to a presidency or deanship, he or she enters a new professional group. Like disciplinary scholars, the executives of higher education learn most from one another—not from "scholars of the discipline," not from "executives in other enterprises," but rather from presidents and deans practicing the same art in similar institutions. Although presentations by experts on libraries, collective bargaining, fund raising, management by objectives, and contract learning have great value, professional vitality is best maintained through the sharing of information *within* the professional group. This is the premise of the Leadership Vitality Project.

As professionals *and* executives, we have a dual obligation to maintain our own vitality and to facilitate the revitalization of our associates.

The rave responses by participants in the Leadership Vitality Project suggest that a structured, preplanned exchange of documents, opinions, achievements, and even rough-draft thoughts *among* conferees should be emphasized in agenda for a wide variety of meetings, e.g., for presidents, deans, department chairs, and other executive and academic officers; held nationally, regionally, or within a single institution; focused on administrator development or a substantive issue. The small groups, the swapping of experiences, the candid speculations, the minor side comments—these are the meat of meetings. A sample of reactions to the project emphasizes the point:

"It has been a genuine pleasure to be a part of this growth experience."

"A rewarding and fascinating project."

"The interviews were indeed fun and useful."

"The time spent interviewing was more valuable than all the conferences and meetings I attended in 1978."

"Superb conference ... "

"The elements of group dynamics at work, the free exchange of ideas within general guidelines, the reinforcement of ideas and introduction of new ones, the making of new acquaintances and friendships, were all very strong and positive elements of this conference."

"Timely and valuable for me. In an age when changing jobs appears to be almost impossible, it is important to find ways for renewal while on the job. You found it."

"It was challenging and inspiring to share ideas with the presidents and vice presidents from so many different institutions. I think most of us are tired of hearing some expert out of Washington come in to lecture to us, and this sharing approach was much more productive."

"It was the best workshop I have attended in my ten years of academic administration."

Formats for Participation

Fortunately, the Leadership Vitality format is easily adapted to other settings, topics, and groups. The common ingredient is a shared commitment to swap information. Swapping tends to be more helpful when "paper" is exchanged, when topics are announced in advance, when groups are twelve persons or fewer, when participants are concerned about similar problems, when group discussion of a single contribution takes place within specified time limits, when participants have grown to know and trust one another, and when a chair accepts responsibility for moving the group along.

The two-hour Leadership Vitality Roundtables (during the annual meetings of the American Council on Education, the Association of American Colleges, the American Association for Higher Education, and the National Association of State Universities and Land-Grant Colleges) covered topics identified by interviewers responding to the instruction, "Check the roundtable topics that would be most useful to you and the topics to which you could make a helpful contribution." The list included about twenty-five possible topics.

Two favorites, "Decision-making Principles" and "Techniques for Evaluating Administrators," were chosen for the roundtable held in conjunction with the AAC meeting. All interviewers and interviewees were invited to attend. Fourteen accepted. Each participant received an advance request to bring fourteen copies of a paragraph-length statement of a favorite "Decision-making Principle" (a paragraph on the *trust theory* was enclosed as an example) and "some paper" concerning administrator evaluation (a form used at Miami University was sent as an example).

The roundtable convened over Dutch-treat breakfast in the convention hotel at 7:15 A.M. Seating was at two seven-person tables. Discussion leaders were instructed to solicit self-introductions (including "the statement of a major leadership challenge just behind or ahead"), to determine how many participants brought handouts on each topic, to apportion forty-five minutes to presentations by participants who brought handouts on the first topic (urging those who forgot handouts to make presentations when time permitted), to summarize the major insights flowing from discussion of the first topic, and to repeat the format for the second topic. Just prior to adjournment at 9:00 A.M., the leaders from each table summarized their table's conversations for the benefit of the other table.

At the roundtables of other meetings, participants used the preadjournment time to present "canned" materials that they had found useful, for example, Alan Lakein's film on time management, *The Time of Your Life*, and Rosabeth Moss Kanter's audiovisual presentation on discrimination, "The Tale of O." Five-minute reviews of T. A. Harris's *I'm O.K., You're O.K.* and Theodore Caplow's *How to Manage Any Organization* fit this same "end of the session" slot.

Of course, more sharing can occur when more time is available. The Leadership Vitality Conference, held June 17–20, 1979, provides a model for two- or three-day meetings. The conference drew thirty-four presidents and chief academic officers with the theme "learn from one another." At the opening session, on Sunday evening, the "you must share" and "you are the experts" and "there really aren't any outside speakers" theme was stressed. Participants were urged to keep a set of "action notes" and to answer Question 10 on leadership qualities. The answers of conference participants were compared with the answers of participants in previous conferences and of national interviewees.

At breakfast each morning at 8:00 A.M., each participant was assigned to a three-person table and given a specific role as interviewer, interviewee, or convenor. Each morning the triad changed but in a way that allowed each participant to play a different role on each of the three mornings.

The convenor was responsible for eliciting ten-minute self-introductions including such topics as "my major achievements since assuming the presidency" or "what my institution and its problems are really like." At 8:30 A.M., the interviewer asked the interviewee a series of questions, first on background (Appendix A, Questions 1–7), then on "educational principles" (Monday interviews) or "implementation strategies" (Tuesday interviews) or "revitalization strategies" (Wednesday interviews).

At 9:30 A.M., the results of the national interviews were presented by lecture. For example, the materials from chapter 2 were presented after the questioning on "Decision-making Principles."

At 10:30 A.M., roundtables were formed. Here, about ten people, each drawn from different triads and grouped by institutional similarity, were asked to share (about ten minutes each) "an insight, conviction, or problem" on the topic of the morning (e.g., Decision-making Principles). Shared were elements of the breakfast conversations, disagreements with the lecture presentation, and personal views.

The morning sessions were the focal point, the highest rated segment of a highly rated conference.

In one of the afternoon sessions, participants were asked to advertise "help available." In five minutes, they shared some topic of recent concern or some expertise that "you are willing to share informally with your colleagues." (Participants could be alerted in advance and encouraged to bring "some paper" for sharing with other participants.)

In another afternoon session, "help wanted" ads were run. Participants were asked to "state a challenge upon which I could use some helpful advice." Again, the statement had to be brief and discussion limited so that other participants could subsequently share their insights with the advice-seeker.

Also, a topic-focused roundtable (on resource reallocation) was held, and films were shown to stimulate group discussion. During breaks, participants were encouraged to browse over "a miscellany of speeches, documents, tapes, policy statements, and helpful journal articles" that had been solicited from national interviewers. Participants could sign up on a buck slip to reserve materials for postconference reading.

The final conference session, in roundtable groups of ten, urged participants to share tentative statements of what had been learned and what changes or plans were contemplated.

Although the Leadership Vitality Conference format is easily adapted to a single day and to almost any topic or group, even a day is not always possible. Sometimes two hours seems like too much time. Yet, it is still possible to pursue the learn-from-other-doers philosophy. Why not urge the chair of the statewide dean's conference to set aside the last hour of a day-long committee meeting for a roundtable on What's Ahead for Me? (More people will stay until the end of the meeting.) Why not begin each vice president's meeting with a ten-minute presentation by one of the groups on "what I learned at my last national meeting" or "new developments in my area" or "here's a practice that I've found helpful"? Why not work such questions into corridor conversations at meetings and into telephone conversations?

The point is that formats can be devised for almost every circumstance. The key is to look upon professional colleagues as major learning resources and to accept a personal obligation for drawing helpful knowledge from them. Professionals operating at the frontier of experience and knowledge must help one another if the state of the art is to be advanced.

Appendix A:

Interview Guide

To: LEADERSHIP VITALITY INTERVIEWERS
From: David G. Brown

You have three copies of this interview guide. It will probably be easiest for you to take notes on the guide itself, dictate from your notes, and send me both your dictation and "scratched on" guide.

As you approach the interview, *please:*

1. Familiarize the interviewee with the project.

2. Answer any questions the interviewee might have about the project.

3. Start through the questionnaire, taking notes as you go.

The questionnaire is divided into four sections:

Section I covers background facts. This section should take no more than fifteen minutes.

Section II focuses on "the meaning and manifestation of effective leadership." I recommend that you spend no more than one hour and fifteen minutes on this section. Remember that the objective of this section is to make more understandable statements such as "an effective leader has a sense of direction" by portraying what a "sense of direction" really is, what "educational principles" are actually applied, what "administrative principles" are in fact used, etc.

Section III concentrates on personal development strategies. Here, the objective is to collect information on the techniques being used to keep up. Allow about an hour for this section.

Section IV is intended to capture information about ideas and specific techniques that we might use. It's the most open-ended portion of the study. I will be interested to see what we get here.

When administering the questionnaire, remember that our main objective is the sharing of information between interviewer and interviewee. The interview is more likely to be a dialogue. Conversation will likely be a shared one. But don't get so interested that you forget to take notes.

Please seek answers to all questions except the optional ones. Questions 9, 11, 13, and 15 are optional.

Good luck.

Sample Interview Guide

Section I: Background information (about 15 minutes)

1. How old are you?

2. How many years have you been on your current job? at your current institution?

3. What job did you hold previously (at the same or different institution)? How long?

4. In what field is your disciplinary training?

5. Since you have become president (provost), has the annual increase in your budget been negative or negligible? 1–10 percent? Over 10 percent?

6. What, if any, formal training have you received in administration (e.g., doctoral discipline, president's institute, special workshop, internship)?

7. What are two or three of your proudest achievements as president (provost)?

Section II: Thoughts on effective leadership (about 1 hour and 15 minutes)

8. Will you share with me your thoughts on *effective leadership?* (15 minutes maximum)

9. *Possible* follow-up questions (use as you wish; about 45 minutes):

   a) Where is your institution heading? Is the direction appropriate? Is the direction new? Does the direction match your aspirations as a leader?

   b) Identify one, two, or three fundamental *educational* principles (e.g., tenets of an educational philosophy) that tend to be reflected in most of your initiatives and decisions (e.g., "a sense of trust must precede educational growth," "students' needs first," "no one best way to education").

   c) Identify and describe one, two, or three fundamental *administrative* principles (i.e., organizational concepts) that tend to be reflected in how you get things done (e.g., "always be optimistic," "delegate and live with results," "respect institutional momentum").

d) Describe a specific problem you solved. How were *you* involved in the solution?

e) Identify one, two, or three principles from your academic discipline that you apply regularly in making decisions (e.g., cost-benefit analysis, comparative advantage, burden of proof, analogy).

10. Twelve leadership qualities are identified, in three major categories. A brief description of each quality appears below.

   You are asked to distribute 100 "weighting points" among the twelve qualities shown on the scoring chart (next page). We suggest that you first distribute 100 points among the three major categories and then subdivide.

Qualities of an Effective Leader

1. *Thinks future possibilities.* The leader relates decisions to a sense of where the college is headed, what it might be ten years from now (e.g., college will become a major research university; college will become a center for adult, part-time learning; private college will become public).

2. *Recognizes present momentum.* The leader relates decisions to the historical strengths of the college, to the convictions of those who populate the institution, to a realistic assessment of current circumstances (educational, fiscal, geographic), to a sense of where the college has been (e.g., college was a normal school, university has been strong in plastics research for three decades, biological science departments are proudly separate).

3. *Owns educational convictions.* The leader relates decisions to three or four general principles about how students learn, what roles are appropriate for colleges, what kinds of knowledge should be part of every curriculum, or how faculty relates to the college mission, etc. (e.g., students learn best in a trust-filled setting, colleges make learning resources more readily available, academic freedom is essential to the critical process).

4. *Thinks globally.* The leader analyzes decisions by thinking bigger—longer terms, higher principle, broader categories, wider geography, etc. (e.g., implications of precedent setting are considered, cost of maintenance is added to cost of purchase, larger risks are taken, effect of local decision on the environment is queried, recommended solution is compared with solution in another culture).

5. *Relates personal values.* The leader relates decisions to a personal respect for all mankind, a conviction that people are more important than procedures, etc. (e.g., honesty, regard for all people, people have a right to know).

Qualities of Effective Leadership—Scoring Chart

	Absurd Illustration	*Your Weights*	*Do this column first*
An effective leader:			
1. Thinks future possibilities	0		
2. Recognizes future possibilities	15		
3. Has educational convictions	0		
4. Thinks globally	0		
5. Relates personal values	0		
1–5 Provides a *sense of direction*	15		
6. Respects expertise in others	5		
7. Recognizes right time and place	5		
8. Understands campus ethos	5		
9. Implements by increments	5		
6–9 Provides a *structure for implementation*	20		
10. Thinks positively	0		
11. Acts with energy	55		
12. Possesses interpersonal skills	10		
10–12 Provides a *sense of enthusiasm*	65		
1–12 Total	100	100 100	100

6. *Respects expertise in others.* The leader listens, consults, delegates, recognizes self-limits, decentralizes, works effectively through others.

7. *Recognizes right time and place.* The leader alters methods and assigns weights to concerns after assessing the particular situation, worries about good timing, decides promptly unless there are reasons to delay, and understands the context of decisions.

8. *Understands campus ethos.* The leader minimizes faux pas by recognizing the decentralized authority structure of colleges, knowing that leading is with the consent of the governed, understanding the informal power structure, sensing the difference between managing a business and administering a college.

9. *Implements by increments.* The leader breaks tasks into achievable steps, bounces back from temporary setbacks, appreciates that slow change is progress, relishes partial successes, avoids ultimatums, avoids becoming dogmatically wed to his or her way, encourages and praises alternative and even contradictory approaches, demonstrates relentless patience.

10. *Thinks positively.* The leader demonstrates great self-respect, discerns the best in everyone and every circumstance, redirects thinking from problems to challenges, builds self-respect in others.

11. *Acts with energy.* The leader is an exemplar of commitment, drive, enthusiasm.

12. *Possesses interpersonal skills.* The leader motivates others, nurtures self-respect in associates, uses humor effectively, empathizes with associates, projects charisma.

11. Possible follow-up questions (use as you wish).

   a) Please check the three qualities that you feel are your strengths.

   b) Please mark with a *W* the two qualities that you feel are your weakest.

Section III: Personal development strategies (about one hour)

12. Will you share with me your thoughts on personal development strategies, on remaining vital as a leader? (15 minutes maximum)

13. Possible follow-up questions (use as you wish).

   a) Whose ideas or concepts have influenced you most during the past several years? What is the relationship of this person to you? (trustee? colleague president? staff member? superior? speaker? guest on campus? colleague in the community? old friend and colleague? spouse?) What was the idea or concept? Where (in what setting and context) did this idea surface? Are there other such incidents you can relate?

b) Is there a person you can bounce ideas off?

c) Do you consciously and intentionally set aside specific times, or a specific time, to rethink big principles, to chart basic directions, etc.? If so, will you describe what you do as preparation for this time? What is the format of the outcome? annual report? position paper?

d) To what extent do you regard professional activities (writing about leadership, attending conferences and colloquia with other presidents and deans, accepting offices in national and regional associations) as an important component of remaining vital? Can you elaborate?

e) What reading (e.g., book, journal, newsletter, newspaper) do you find most useful to your leadership responsibility? What three items would you recommend for reading to colleague presidents or provosts?

f) Do you think it necessary to get off campus in order to gain perspective on what's happening on campus? What percentage of your work time do you spend off campus?

g) In what ways, subtle and overt, have you changed your leadership as times have moved from expansion to stability?

h) Can you give an example of a matter on which you changed your mind, and explain why?

i) How closely do you maintain a link to your discipline? Do you teach? write? attend annual meetings?

j) What are some of your suggestions for maintaining the vitality and vibrancy of an institution and its leaders? (e.g., periodic evaluation, term appointments, sabbaticals, creation of a place with prestige to move tired presidents, board of educational advisers, enrollment in college courses.)

k) How long can a president or chief academic officer remain effective?

Section IV: Tips on effective administration (about an hour and a half)

14. What *specific* tips on "how to get the leadership job done" can you think of?

15. Possible follow-up questions (use as you wish):

   a) What are some time-feasible suggestions for administrator self-development? Do you have specific suggestions about reading habits? convention-going habits? workshop attendance?

   b) What techniques and procedures of effective administration do you use that you feel could be used by others? (e.g., Do you use a special search committee procedure? Do you have a special way to relate to the board? Are there special techniques for keeping in touch with the campus?)

Appendix B:

Hypotheses on Effective Leadership

1. An effective leader thinks future possibilities

A leader relates decisions to a sense of direction, of where the college is headed (e.g., the college will become a major research university, the college will become a center for adult, part-time learning, the sponsorship of the college will shift from private to public).

2. An effective leader recognizes the present momentum of the college

A leader uses the institution's power, its momentum . . . what the college is and where it is headed.

3. An effective leader has, and consistently applies, educational convictions

- An effective leader has a well-formulated educational philosophy.
- An effective leader has a clear sense of priorities.
- An effective leader is persistent.
- An effective leader apportions time according to problems to be solved, not people to be seen.
- Has one's field of professional training any bearing on one's success or style as an administrator? (Rhoten A. Smith)
- Discipline and professional field are essentially irrelevant; some able administrators come from "relevant" fields such as public administration, law, etc., while others come from "irrelevant" fields such as philosophy and the sciences. (Robert M. O'Neil)

- There will be a reasonably clear sense of priorities—things which the administrator would at least like to be able to do, though the ability to implement the goals may be limited in practice. (Robert M. O'Neil)
- How much impact can or does a leader have in trying to maintain or improve the educational standards of his institution? (Robert E. Wolverton)
- Don't be afraid to use judgment; i.e., don't rely on data and formulas as crutches. Administrators are paid to exercise judgment and I think most faculty and staff expect and respect informed judgment. (Melvin D. George)

4. An effective leader thinks globally

- An effective leader thinks big (longer term, higher principles, broader generalities).
- An effective leader is less parochial in background.
- An effective leader sees and conveys patterns of decision.
- An effective leader thinks ecologically or in terms of relationships.
- An effective leader thinks continually about theories of leadership.
- Successful presidents have noted that "the theory and practice of managing higher education institutions has changed significantly in the past ten to fifteen years" (Harold Howe II, "The President's Role," *Leadership for Higher Education: The Campus View*, ed. R. W. Heyns, American Council on Education, 1977, p. 12). The presumption here is that successful presidents see that they must make important contributions to the capacity of institutions to meet their fiscal problems and to operate efficiently; to utilize offices of institutional research and to apply modern technologies and concepts to the management of their institutions. A further note, however, from Howe's commentary: "The tragedy of today's presidency is that circumstances conspire to deny colleges and universities the most important contributions their presidents can make," i.e., becoming so immersed in all the new systems of control and planning that independent thinking about educational issues is left by the wayside. (Leslie F. Malpass)
- Successful presidents are very bright, articulate, well read, catholic in their interests and tastes, and insightful about state and national events of significance not only to higher education but to the general population as well. (Leslie F. Malpass)

5. An effective leader relates personal values to decision making

- An effective leader has integrity.
- An effective leader is dependable, predictable.
- An effective leader has credibility fostered by a coherent perspective leading to consistency, leading to integrity, and therefore leading to credibility.
- An effective leader emphasizes the human dimension first.
- An effective leader deals with people as equals.
- An effective leader teaches periodically to reestablish credibility.
- An effective leader has a self-image of a faculty member turned administrator.
- Be kind, even when being hard-nosed. A university is, after all, a people place, and one can be humane without being weak. (Melvin D. George)
- In their hearts, would they rather be doing something else? (Franklin W. Wallin)

6. An effective leader respects expertise in others

- An effective leader strongly respects existing faculty and student governance systems.
- An effective leader believes in the supremacy of the faculty in matters of its expertise on most educational matters.
- An effective leader knows the limits of his or her own skill and authority.
- The president or the academic vice president can at best be a coordinator of academic and faculty affairs, not an intellectual leader. The specialization of knowledge and the highly individual nature of scholarship make it impossible for an academic leader to be an intellectual leader, except in relation to the higher education enterprise as an enterprise. (John D. Millett)
- An effective leader is sensitive to the ideas, convictions, and feelings of others.
- An effective leader listens well.
- An effective leader handles well things initiated by others.
- An effective leader is reactive.
- Has leadership become so multifaceted that "a leader" really needs an administrative team which agrees to a level of 80 percent on the goals or objectives of the institution *and* on the strategies and tactics to achieve them? (Robert E. Wolverton)

- Effective leadership occurs where real authority is delegated and those to whom it is delegated feel a very real sense of freedom to make the decisions and to assume responsibility for those decisions. (Nash N. Winstead)
- Successful presidents delegate operational activities to competent deputies and spend a reasonable amount of time reflecting about and attempting to implement their institution's basic missions and objectives. (Leslie F. Malpass)
- Survival as an academic leader is based primarily on delegation of responsibility to appropriate staff. A president must accept and have confidence in recommendations of key colleagues—even if he or she believes they are incorrect.
- Seek advice freely and with an open mind, and try to let people know why their advice was not taken. If you've already made up your mind about an item, it's very difficult to ask for counsel without revealing that your mind is closed. People resent being asked to give advice for form's sake only and on many occasions the advice is worth hearing. (Melvin D. George)
- An effective leader supports his or her subordinates.
- An effective leader has an ability to work through others.
- An effective leader delegates and gives subordinates a real sense of freedom.
- An effective leader has an ability to structure problems, meetings, and decisions so that responsibility may be allocated to associates.
- An effective leader delegates only the authority to advise the decision.
- What is the design behind the assignments of specific functions in those who report to the particular officer? Will these assignments be distinct and separate from each other, or is there an intentional overlapping requiring subordinates to work together? In other words, what mechanism is used by the administrative officer to encourage major staff to cooperate and collaborate? (Nash N. Winstead)
- What can be learned about a president or chief academic officer by observing and evaluating the caliber of his staff? (Rhoten A. Smith)
- Success can be achieved if loyalty can be built both ways—up and down the organization chart. If a person feels he or she will be trusted to do a job, then the leader can expect the same treatment. (Harry A. Marmion)
- Don't ask for reports or reviews without letting people know what has happened as a result. It is demoralizing for a committee to submit a report or for a program to undergo an intensive review and then have only magnificent silence from on high as the result. Faculty and staff are entitled to some response in such instances, and future cooperation will be considerably harder to come by without it. (Melvin D. George)

- An effective leader regularly communicates with internal constituencies in a more or less formal manner.
- An effective leader is more a politician, manager, mediator, and chair than an entrepreneur, anarchist, catalyst, judge, philosopher-king.
- Respect is all one can hope for in a position of academic leadership, and it can only be achieved by (1) openness in discussion of important issues, seeking the widest range of constituent opinion, and (2) willingness to admit mistakes or errors and be able to say, "I was wrong, I blew it, that was a mistake"; the assurance that judgments will be made on the merits, not on politics. (Harry A. Marmion)

7. An effective leader recognizes that different situations call for different actions

- An effective leader frequently articulates consensus as an expected part of the job.
- An effective leader anticipates consensus by stating it so that others may rally 'round.
- An effective leader has a mediative view.
- An effective leader varies techniques according to the situation.
- An effective leader realizes that leadership skills that are right for one situation are sometimes wrong for another.
- An effective leader is sometimes made to look horrible, wonderful, by the circumstance rather than by skill.
- Leadership does require adaptive techniques because of the constituencies we must work with and convince. (Robert E. Wolverton)
- We should avoid talking about leadership as if it were a clearly definable quality with standardized dimensions. A successful leader in one situation can fall flat on his face in another. (Frederic W. Ness)
- An able administrator can, of course, alter the situation in which he or she must function, but I believe (hypothesize) that there are some important personal characteristics needed which cannot be built into organizational or institutional process. (Robert G. Arns)
- I'd like to discover the relative role of the person and the situation, and the extent to which the balance depends on the individual officer. (Robert G. Arns)

8. An effective leader understands the campus ethos

- An effective leader understands and accepts the unique characteristics of the university as an organized enterprise.

- An effective leader walks the campus.
- An effective leader knows and uses leverage.
- An effective leader knows the power base (budget, academic expertise, administrative finesse, charisma, institutional) and uses it.
- The study should analyze any variations that we find in the source of power for academic leadership. Is it based on academic expertise or prowess? Is it based on budget control? Is it based on administrative skill and finesse? Is it based on the individual's personality—magnetic, dynamic, brilliant, or creative? (Nash N. Winstead)
- There frequently are *institutional* power sources which can be utilized by leaders, thereby demanding less reliance on personal power sources. (Robert E. Wolverton)
- Operate within established governance procedures and use established committees whenever possible. The creation of a lot of ad hoc committees is, in my opinion, not a sound administrative practice. If you have too many such groups, it may indicate a weakness in the regular governance system. Generally, conclusions and recommendations may have more validity if they come through established channels. (Melvin D. George)
- An effective leader understands that faculty make policy and leaders refine it.
- An effective leader realizes that service is with consent, though not always approval, of the governed.
- An effective leader appreciates and honors decentralization as a distinctive feature of the organization called a college.
- An effective leader emphasizes the grass roots.
- There will be a strong respect for the existing faculty and student governance systems, whether or not the administrator is the presiding officer. (Robert M. O'Neil)
- An effective leader recognizes that the skills for managing a business enterprise differ from those for administering colleges.
- Academic leaders can be "successful" (whatever that means) only to the extent they understand and accept the unique characteristics of the university as an organized enterprise. (John D. Millett)
- An effective leader has faculty background.
- The growing lack of consensus within each of our major constituencies makes leadership more difficult to exercise. (Robert E. Wolverton)
- There will be a pattern of regular communication with faculty, staff, and other internal constituencies (in a more or less formal manner). (Robert M. O'Neil)
- I would suggest that you do some study of the contrasting leadership styles that I would characterize as the push versus the pull approach. (Nash N. Winstead)

9. *An effective leader implements by increments*

- An effective leader asks many questions but makes few irrevocable statements.
- An effective leader is adaptable, flexible, accommodating.
- An effective leader sees the university as a "wiggly" world with many ambiguities and many unresolvable complexities.
- An effective leader recognizes his or her ability to be wrong, especially when others disagree.
- An effective leader can accept criticism.
- An effective leader is willing to reverse a decision.
- An effective leader is willing to pursue several channels to get the job done.
- An effective leader has a pragmatic, problem-solving style that stresses compromise, assimilation, adaptation, and the value of coalition.
- An effective leader has a long fuse.
- An effective leader encourages the development of many alternatives and broad participation.
- An effective leader is open, nondefensive.
- An effective leader acts incrementally, not monumentally.
- An effective leader has a sense of direction, not a precise destination.
- An effective leader has a high tolerance for ambiguity and ability to deal with it.
- An effective leader believes that "education is hanging around until you have caught on."

10. *An effective leader thinks positively*

- An academic leader must project an image that instills confidence in his or her decisions on the part of a variety of constituencies, both internal and external to the institution served.
- An effective leader is an enthusiastic supporter.
- An effective leader has high self-respect and humility.
- An effective leader admits mistakes and tolerates self-failures.
- An effective leader seeks a periodic review of performance by faculty and students.
- An effective leader doesn't take things personally but rather sees himself or herself as part of a system.
- An effective leader always has a positive perspective.
- An effective leader escapes becoming cynical, insensitive, paranoid.
- Successful academic leaders should have a background as successful scholars. (Lloyd I. Watkins)

- Remember that a sense of well being and worth among faculty and staff is at least as important as salary levels. Make people feel important, recognize their achievements and encourage them in their failings.
- Leaders inevitably become cynical and paranoid; it is only a matter of time.

11. An effective leader acts with energy

- An effective leader advocates fearlessly.
- An effective leader initiates more than responds.
- An effective leader manages unobtrusively.
- An effective leader seeks a low profile.
- An effective leader is energetic.
- An effective leader is intelligent.
- An effective leader thrives in the job.
- An effective leader is committed to training younger and potential administrators.
- An effective leader sets an example of dedication and enthusiasm.
- An effective leader persists.
- An effective leader spends time.
- There will be a strong commitment to initiation rather than response; in terms of calendar, communications, and other indicia, the major emphasis will be on initiating rather than responding. (Robert M. O'Neil)
- In plain English, a president must project an image of leadership on any issue he comes into contact with that is associated with college or community (including even tennis). (Harry A. Marmion)
- Make a decision promptly or let the parties know that no decision will be made. I think one of the biggest failings of academic administrators and one of the things most resented by faculty and staff is a decision process that drags on and on. It is appropriate not to make a decision about something on occasion, but the parties have a right to know that a decision will be postponed and to know why. (Melvin D. George)

12. An effective leader possesses interpersonal skills

- An effective leader exudes caring.
- An effective leader needs interpersonal relations skills more than managerial skills.
- An effective leader has a sense of humor and uses humor effectively.
- An effective leader communicates well.

- An effective leader regards people as more important than procedures.
- An effective leader communicates, listens, develops a feeling for people's style of truth telling.
- An effective leader gives early signals in order to avoid confrontation.
- An effective leader uses mechanisms to encourage associates to work together.
- An effective leader communicates well.
- An effective leader constantly works to keep all communication channels open and unclogged by trivia.
- An effective leader gives credit to others.
- An effective leader sacrifices status for substance.
- Interpersonal relations are more essential to the success of a president or chief academic officer than are managerial skills. (Mary S. Metz)

American Council on Education

The American Council on Education, founded in 1918 and composed of institutions of higher education and national and regional education associations, is the nation's major nongovernmental coordinating body for postsecondary education. Through voluntary and cooperative action, the Council provides comprehensive leadership for improving educational standards, services, policies, and procedures.